SOLUTIONS
TO EXERCISES

INTRODUCTION
TO LOGIC   FIFTH EDITION

Irving M. Copi University of Hawaii

MACMILLAN PUBLISHING CO., INC.
New York
COLLIER MACMILLAN PUBLISHERS
London

Macmillan Publishing Co., Inc.
866 Third Avenue, New York, New York 10022

Collier Macmillan Canada, Ltd.

ISBN 0-02-324890-4

Printing: 1 2 3 4 5 6 7 8   Year: 8 9 0 1 2 3 4

PREFACE

This little book contains answers to most of the exercises
in INTRODUCTION TO LOGIC, Fifth Edition. It does not, of course,
repeat the answers given in the back of the textbook itself. Nor
does it offer solutions for all of the exercises in Chapters 11,
12, and 13, for those require longer verbal answers than can be
included in a solutions manual of this type. But the illustra-
tive discussions in the text should enable teachers to evaluate
their students' answers without too much difficulty. The formal
proofs of validity given here are neither the only ones nor the
shortest ones possible, and for some proofs of invalidity not
all truth value assignments are included. One final remark
concerning the exercises on analyzing, recognizing, and classi-
fying arguments (Chapter 1), on language functions and kinds of
agreement and disagreement (Chapter 2), on informal fallacies
(Chapter 3), on verbal disputes and on the criticism and discussion of definitions (Chapter 4): I have given what seem to
me to be the best answers, but ingenious students continually
surprise me with a variety of alternative answers for which
plausible justifications can be supplied, and I think it is
entirely proper to "give credit" for analyses and solutions
that a student can defend.

2. Premisses: (1) Employers, emerging from a recession, usually expand hours for their existing workers before they hire new ones. (2) The average quality of those unemployed declines as the better educated among them are rehired first. (3) These two factors combine to reduce the leverage of economic growth on the unemployment rate.
   Conclusion: A growth rate of five per cent would reduce the unemployment rate by only one-third of a percentage point.
3. Premisses: (1) The Fourteenth Amendment was deliberately formulated to prohibit precisely such classifications on the basis of race, for purposes of law school admission and the like. (2) The Constitution is and always must be, in that sense, color blind. (3) [The Constitution] cannot be, from time to time and at the discretion of certain agencies or administrators, color conscious in order to become color blind at some future date. (4) The principle that a person's race is simply not relevant in the application of the laws is a treasured one.
   Conclusion: Classifications on the basis of race, for purpose of law school admission and the like, are per se unconstitutional.
4. Premisses: (1) Today, any able-bodied American high school graduate with a C average during his junior and senior years can gain admittance to some American college or university if he really tries. (2) When parents can not or will not pay all the costs, the government or a scholarship of some sort will help.
   Conclusion: A student can now consider a college education almost as much a right as free speech.
6. Premiss: Large numbers of people in this country have never had to deal with the criminal justice system.
   Conclusion: Large numbers of people in this country are unaware of how the criminal justice system works and of the extraordinarily detrimental impact it has upon many people's lives.
7. Premisses: (1) To determine an electron's orbit one would shine light on the electron. (2) But the light's quanta have energy and momentum, and if one attempts to "see" an atomic electron by shining light on it, the light's quanta transfer so much momentum to the electron that it is knocked clear out of the atom.
   Conclusion: Therefore, the electron's orbit cannot be determined.
8. Premisses: (1) In the case of a "war for limited objectives" the historian can hope to specify causes

1

with some precision; he begins his inquiry from the stated war aims. (2) But in a "total war" stated war aims are 'vague and comprehensive and they are not intended to limit the actions of their author.

Conclusion: So the historian can only say that such a war was caused by the whole situation preceding it.

9. Premiss: Philosophy resting on badly understood science is almost as bad as philosophy that ignores science altogether.

Conclusion: When one makes use of scientific results in philosophical analyses, one had better be sure that he has got the science right.

11. Premisses: (1) The pattern of female employment follows the course of the role that women play outside industry. (2) Women are almost always ancillary, handmaids in the more important work of men.

Conclusion: Equal pay for equal work will not make as great a difference as women might hope in these figures--that the average male employee in the United States earns $6,610 a year; his sister $3,157, less than half.

12. Premisses: (1) Business cycles, large and small, appear to be a continuing feature of the economic landscape. (2) A turn up or down in the economy is clearly an event of major social significance.

Conclusion: Considerable interest attaches to the means whereby an economic turn can be forecast and its extent can be estimated.

13. Premisses: (1) Poetry expresses the universal. (2) History expresses only the particular.

Conclusion: Poetry is finer and more philosophical than history.

14. Premisses: (1) Venus and Mercury never move far away from the sun. (2) Venus and Mercury are now seen beyond the sun and now on this side of it.

Conclusion: Venus and Mercury revolve around the sun.

16. Premisses: (1) Any attempt to base logical principles on something more ultimate, whether it be our system of contingent rules for the use of language or anything else, consists of deducing conclusions from premisses. (2) For deduction to be possible the prior validity of logical laws is a prerequisite.

Conclusion: Any attempt to base logical principles on something more ultimate, whether it be our system of contingent rules for the use of language or anything else, must be self-defeating.

17. Premisses: (1) Tourism [in Egypt] should normally earn $100 million a year with such attractions as the pyramids, the Sphinx, and other pharaonic tombs and temples. (2) Britain has imposed tight currency controls on its tourists. (3) West Germany dis-

2

courages its vacationers from going to Egypt because
Cairo broke diplomatic relations over Bonn's recognition of Israel. (4) Big-spending Americans are
fed up with second-class hotels, shoddy service,
and foul food.
Conclusion: Earnings [of tourism in Egypt] this year
will be only about $40 million.

18. Premisses: (1) Through their pension funds, employees
of American business own today at least 25 per cent
of the equity capital of American business. (2)
The pension funds of the self-employed, of public
employees, and of school and college teachers own
at least another 10 per cent more, giving the
workers of America ownership of more than one third
of the equity capital of American business. (3)
Within another 10 years the pension funds inevitably
will increase their holdings and will, by 1985 at
the latest, own at least 50 per cent of the equity
capital of American business. (4) And all of this,
of course, excludes personal ownership of stock by
individual American workers--a small, but not neg-
ligible, percentage of the total.
Conclusion: If "socialism" is defined as "ownership of
the means of production by the workers"--and this
is the orthodox definition--then the United States
is the most "socialist" country in the world.

19. Premiss: Discontent with one's condition amidst the
press of worries and unsatisfied wants may easily
become a great temptation to the transgression of
duties.
Conclusion: To safeguard one's happiness is a duty,
at least indirectly.

21. Premisses: (1) During the school period the student has
been mentally bending over his desk. (2) At the
University he should stand up and look around.
Conclusion: It is fatal if the first year at the University be frittered away in going over the old
work in the old spirit.

22. Premiss: Citizens who so value their "independence" that
they will not enroll in a political party...abandon
a share in decision-making at the primary level:
the choice of the candidate.
Conclusion: Citizens who so value their "independence"
that they will not enroll in a political party are
really forfeiting independence.

23. Premiss: [If we do not know any of the facts about the
subject on which we are to speak and argue then]
we can have no materials out of which to construct
arguments.
Conclusion: Whether our argument concerns public affairs
or some other subject we must know some, if not all,

3

of the facts about the subject on which we are to
speak and argue.

24. Premisses: (1) Happiness consists in peace of mind.
(2) Durable peace of mind depends on the confidence
we have in the future. (3) That confidence is
based on the science we should have of the nature
of God and the soul.
Conclusion: Science is necessary for true happiness.

25. Premisses: (1) First, the personality and character--
which are really synonymous--take their form during
the first six or eight years of life. (2) During
this period of infancy and childhood, we select and
develop the techniques which gain us satisfaction,
defend us against threats, and become the tools in
coping with the endless variety of problem situations that will be encountered later in life. (3)
It is during this time that we develop our methods
of relating ourselves to other people and undergo
the experiences which determine the strength and
weaknesses within our personality. (4) As adults
we are not able to remember the details of these
formative years.
Conclusion: Therefore, we cannot understand our own
behavior fully.

26. Premiss: (1) A girl's intellect ripens faster [than a
boy's].
Conclusion: If there were to be any difference between
a girl's education and a boy's, I should say that
of the two the girl should be earlier led into deep
and serious subjects: and that her range of lit-
erature should be, not more, but less frivolous.

27. Premisses: (1) All censorships exist to prevent anyone
from challenging current conceptions and existing
institutions. (2) All progress is initiated by
challenging current conceptions, and executed by
supplanting existing institutions.
Conclusion: The first condition of progress is the
removal of censorships.

28. Premiss: Every art and every inquiry, and similarly
every action and pursuit, is thought to aim at some
good.
Conclusion: The good has rightly been declared to be
that at which all things aim.

29. Premiss: Everybody thinks himself so abundantly provided
with good sense that even those most difficult to
please in all other matters do not commonly desire
more of it than they already possess.
Conclusion: Good sense is of all things in the world
the most equally distributed.

30. Premisses: (1) If protesters did feel that the law is

4

sacred, any deliberate infringement--whether by
Dr. Spock, a Black Power agitator, a striking
garbage collector, or a driver risking a parking
ticket--would involve them in a tragic conflict,
genre of Corneille: Love versus Duty. (2) Among
infringers, I see a good deal of calculation of
consequences, and on the part of Dr. Spock, Dr.
King, and others, an admirable courage and patriotism; but I have not seen any signs of inner
tragic conflict.
Conclusion: Certainly, protesters do not _feel_ that the
law is sacred.

Exercises on pages 17-22
2. First argument:
    Premiss: Socialism is a system built on belief
        in human goodness.
    Conclusion: Socialism never works.
    Second argument:
    Premiss: Capitalism is a system built on belief
        in human selfishness.
    Conclusion: Given checks and balances, it is
        nearly always a smashing, scandalous success.
3. First argument:
    Premisses: (1) Most people are familiar with the
        sensation of "hunger pangs" which arise
        from the rhythmic contractions of the empty
        stomach. (2) These internal rumblings were
        the first manifestations of hunger to be
        investigated.
    Conclusion: One is hungry because his stomach is
        empty (the "empty stomach" theory of hunger).
    Second argument:
    Premiss: When blood was taken from starving
        dogs and given (via transfusion) to dogs
        who had just finished eating, the "full"
        dogs immediately started to eat again.
    Conclusion: The dogs ate even though their
        stomachs were not empty.
    Third argument:
    Premiss: The preceding conclusion.
    Conclusion: It is not true that one is hungry
        because his stomach is empty (the downfall
        of the "empty stomach" theory).
    Fourth argument:
    Premiss: The preceding conclusion.
    Conclusion: Stomach fullness, therefore, seems
        to play some role in hunger, but, for the
        most part, only a small segment.
4. First argument:
    Premisses: (1) Abstract painting is the attempt

5

to have, in the ordinary sense, no content.
(2) There is no content of abstract painting.
Conclusion: There can be no interpretation of
abstract painting.

Second argument:
Premiss: The preceding conclusion.
Conclusion: The flight from interpretation seems
particularly a feature of modern painting.

6. First argument:
Premiss: The Buddha is everywhere.
Conclusion: To ask the perennial classical
question that asks which part of the motorcycle, which grain of sand in which pile,
is the Buddha, is to look in the wrong
direction.

Second argument:
Premiss: The Buddha is everywhere.
Conclusion: To ask the perennial classic question
that asks which part of the motorcycle,
which grain of sand in which pile, is the
Buddha, is to look in the right direction.

7. First argument:
Premiss: There is dissatisfaction with existing
economic and social arrangements and
conditions.
Conclusion: With a more rational, foresighted
approach to economic life--national plan-
ning--we can do better.

Second argument:
Premiss: One cannot derive the efficacy of policy
B from the deficiency of policy A.
Conclusion: The inference drawn in the first
argument is a logical fallacy.

Third argument:
Premisses: (1) If national economic planning
is desirable public policy, it must be
because it is both conceptually sound and
consistent with the political reality in
which it must necessarily function. (2)
Unfortunately, it is neither.
Conclusion: [not explicitly stated in the cited
passage] National economic planning is not
desirable public policy.

8. First argument:
Premisses: (1) Mr. Grey, the member for Silverbridge, is going to Persia. (2) Mr. Grey
is a Member of Parliament. (3) Members
of Parliament ought to be in London and
not in Persia. (4) It is generally supposed
that no man in England is more prone to do
what he ought to do than Mr. Grey.

Conclusion: Therefore Mr. Grey will cease to be
Member for Silverbridge.

Second Argument:
Premisses: (1) The Duke rules the borough. (2)
The Duke's wife rules the Duke.
Conclusion: Therefore the Duke's wife rules the
borough.

9. First Argument:
Premiss: It is the average person who has at his
disposal the single most important resource
for stopping crime--information.
Conclusion: Neither increases in police patrols
nor harsher treatment by the courts can have
much impact if ordinary people refuse to
get involved.

Second argument:
Premiss: Without the intervention of third par-
ties, there is little chance of rescuing
victims, apprehending criminals, or solving
crimes.
Conclusion: The eyewitness of criminal events
plays an indispensable role in law enforce-
ment.

Third argument:
Premiss: The preceding conclusion.
Conclusion: Therefore, a crucial priority in
criminal justice policy must be to increase
the responsiveness of bystanders when they
confront criminal behavior.

11. First argument:
Premisses: (1) That the people have an original
right to establish, for their future government, such principles as, in their opinion,
shall most conduce to their own happiness
is the basis on which the whole American
fabric has been erected. (2) The exercise
of this original right is a very great
exertion; nor can it, nor ought it, to be
frequently repeated.
Conclusion: The principles, therefore, so
established, are deemed fundamental.

Second argument:
Premisses: (1) The first premiss of the first
argument. (2) The authority from which
these principles proceed is supreme, and
can seldom act.
Conclusion: These principles are designed to be
permanent.

12. First argument:
Premisses: (1) Changing relationships in

production is not enough to change the relationships between individuals. (2) More specifically women have not become the equals of men. in any socialist country what-soever.

Conclusion: Women have seen that socialism has not solved their problems.

Second argument:

Premiss: Many active members of Women's Lib and of the French MLF have first-hand knowledge [that] even in the most authentically re-volutionary groups women are only given the most unpleasant tasks and all the leaders are men.

13. First argument:

Premisses: (1) A virtue is a praiseworthy habit of choice. (2) Neither a substance nor an evidence can be a habit of choice.

Conclusion: Neither a substance nor an evidence can be a virtue.

Second argument:

Premisses: (1) The most famous Christian account of "faith" is that in Heb. xi. 1: "Faith is the substance of things hoped for, the evidence of things not seen." (2) The pre-ceding conclusion.

Conclusion: The most famous Christian account of "faith" does not make faith a virtue.

Third argument:

Premisses: (1) The most famous Christian account of "faith" is obviously unintelligible. (2) The preceding conclusion.

Conclusion: When we investigate what Christians mean by their peculiar use of the word "faith," I think we come to the remarkable conclusion that all their accounts of it are either unintelligible or false.

14. First argument:

Premiss: In a society in which money determines value, women [who perform household labor, including child care] are a group who work outside the money economy.

Conclusion: The work of women [who perform...] is not worth money.

Second argument:

Premiss: The preceding conclusion.

Conclusion: The work of women [who perform...] is therefore valueless.

Third argument:

Premiss: The preceding conclusion.

8

Conclusion: The work of women [who perform...]
is therefore not even real work.
Fourth argument:
Premiss: The conclusion of the second argument
above.
Conclusion: Women themselves, who do this valueless work, can hardly be expected to be worth
as much as men, who work for money.
16. First argument:
Premiss: The machine will not be provided with
legs.
Conclusion: The machine could not be asked to go
out and fill the coal scuttle.
Second argument:
Premisses: (1) The preceding conclusion. (2)
However well these deficiencies [lack of legs,
eyes, etc.] might be overcome by clever en-
gineering, one could not send the creature
to school without the other children making
excessive fun of it.
Conclusion: It will not be possible to apply
exactly the same teaching process to the
machine as to a normal child.
Third argument:
Premiss: The example of Miss Helen Keller shows
that education can take place provided that
communication in both directions between
teacher and pupil can take place by some
means or other.
Conclusion: We need not be too concerned about
the [machine's lack of] legs, eyes, etc.
17. First argument:
Premiss: The nine justices on a single court
cannot arrive at a single definition [of
obscenity] that they can work with, but
consistently come up with as many as seven
or eight separate views on the meaning of
the term in a given case.
Conclusion: If no satisfactory definition of
obscenity has thus far been developed, it
cannot be for lack of effort.
Second argument:
Premiss: If no definition of the key term
(obscenity) can be found, then there is
no way to distinguish obscene materials from
those that are not obscene.
Conclusion: If no definition of the key term
(obscenity) can be found, then it is impossible to inquire meaningfully into the
effects of obscene materials.

Third argument:
    Premisses: (1) The premiss of the first argument.
    (2) The conclusion of the second argument.
    Conclusion: It is obvious that the problem [of
    defining obscenity] is not only a difficult
    one, but that it has serious practical con-
    sequences.
Fourth argument:
    Premiss: The conclusion of the second argument
    above.
    Conclusion: For the student who is interested
    in studying the effects of obscene materials,
    such a state of affairs must be most dis-
    concerting.

18. First argument:
    Premiss: If determinism is true then judgments
    of regret imply that what is impossible
    yet ought to be.
    Conclusion: If determinism is true then judgments
    of regret are pessimistic.
Second argument:
    Premiss: The preceding conclusion.
    Conclusion: If determinism is true then judgments
    of regret are wrong.
Third argument:
    Premisses: (1) The preceding conclusion. (2)
    If judgments of regret are wrong then other
    judgments, judgments of approval presumably,
    ought to be in their place. (3) If deter-
    minism is true then judgments of regret are
    necessitated and nothing else can be in
    their place.
    Conclusion: If determinism is true then the
    universe is a place in which what ought to
    be appears impossible.

19. First argument:
    Premisses: (1) The price of occupational success
    is made so high for women that barring ex-
    ceptional luck only the unusually talented
    or frankly neurotic can afford to succeed.
    (2) Girls size up the bargain early and
    turn it down.
    Conclusion: We are destroying talent.
Second argument:
    Premiss: The able workers that employers say
    they can't find are all too often in their
    own back rooms or lofts doing jobs that use
    only a fraction of their ability.
    Conclusion: We are wasting talent.

Third argument:
     Premiss: Some of our brightest citizens are
          quietly tucked away at home, their aptitudes
          concealed by the label "Housewife."
     Conclusion: We are hiding talent.
21. First argument:
     Premiss: A punishment which comes at the end of
          all things, when the world is over and done
          with, cannot have for its object either to
          improve or deter.
     Conclusion: A punishment which comes at the end
          of all things, when the world is over and
          done with, is pure vengeance.
Second argument:
     Premiss: A punishment which comes at the end of
          all things, when the world is over and done
          with, is pure vengeance.
     Conclusion: God, who prescribes forbearance and
          forgiveness of every fault, exercises none
          himself, but does the exact opposite.
22. First argument:
     Premiss: The right answer given to a teacher's
          question will tell him that his teaching
          is good and that he can go on to the next
          topic.
     Conclusion: A teacher who asks a question is
          tuned to the right answer, ready to hear
          it, eager to hear it.
Second argument:
     Premiss: A teacher who asks a question is tuned
          to the right answer, ready to hear it, eager
          to hear it.
     Conclusion: He will assume that anything that
          sounds close to the right answer is meant
          to be the right answer.
Third argument:
     Premiss: He (the teacher) will assume that any-
          thing that sounds close to the right answer
          is meant to be the right answer.
     Conclusion: For a student who is not sure of the
          answer a mumble may be his best bet.
23. First argument:
     Premisses: (1) If Materialism is true, all our
          thoughts are produced by purely material
          antecedents. (2) Purely material antecedents
          are quite blind, and are just as likely to
          produce falsehood as truth.
     Conclusion: [If Materialism is true] we have no
          reason for believing any of our conclusions--
          including the truth of Materialism.

11

Second argument:
    Premiss: The preceding conclusion.
    Conclusion: Materialism is a self-contradictory hypothesis.

24. First argument:
    Premiss: Hydrogen is being steadily converted into helium throughout the Universe and this conversion is a one-way process--that is to say, hydrogen cannot be produced in any appreciable quantity through the breakdown of the other elements.
    Conclusion: If all the material of the Universe were infinitely old, there could be no hydrogen left in the Universe.

Second argument:
    Premisses: (1) The preceding conclusion. (2) The Universe consists almost entirely of hydrogen.
    Conclusion: It is not possible that all the material of the Universe is infinitely old.

Third argument:
    Premisses: (1) The preceding conclusion. (2) To avoid the issue of creation it would be necessary for all the material of the Universe to be infinitely old.
    Conclusion: It is not possible that the whole question of the creation of the Universe could be avoided in some way.

25. First argument:
    Premiss: The neutrino has no charge and no mass, and it interacts very weakly with ordinary matter.
    Conclusion: The neutrino is almost impossible to detect directly.

Second argument:
    Premisses: (1) Indeed, someone has estimated that if one took a single neutrino produced in the accelerator at CERN or the one at Brookhaven (where the first high-energy neutrino experiments were done) and shot it through a layer of lead about as thick as the distance from here to Pluto, it would undergo only one collision during its entire passage. (2) Fortunately, however, the experimenter is not limited to one neutrino; an accelerator produces millions of them a second.
    Conclusion: Some [neutrinos produced in an accelerator] are bound to make a collision in a target of reasonable size.

EXERCISES ON PAGES 22-26

Third argument:
    Premisses: (1) The conclusion of the preceding
      argument. (2) These collisions produce
      particles that <u>can</u> be seen.
    Conclusion: So neutrino reactions can be studied.
Fourth argument:
    Premiss: Neutrino collisions are so rare.
    Conclusion: The whole experimental area must be
      carefully shielded from cosmic rays and
      other annoying background that could be con-
      fused with the few events that one is looking
      for.

Exercises on pages 26-31

2. First argument:
    Premiss: Invariably, high-status parents will
      seek to pass on their positions either
      through the use of influence or simply by
      the cultural advantages their children would
      possess.
    Conclusion: Thus, after one generation a merito-
      cracy simply becomes an enclaved class.
  Second argument:
    Premiss: The preceding conclusion.
    Conclusion: There never can be a pure meritocracy.

3. First argument:
    Premiss: To separate [Black children] from others
      of similar age and qualifications solely be-
      cause of their race generates a feeling of
      inferiority as to their status in the commu-
      nity that may affect their hearts and minds
      in a way unlikely ever to be undone.
    Conclusion: Separate educational facilities are
      inherently unequal.
  Second argument:
    Premiss: The preceding conclusion.
    Conclusion: We conclude that in the field of
      public education the doctrine of "separate
      but equal" has no place.

4. Argument:
    Premisses: (1) Often exams are treated as
      obstacles to be overcome rather than as
      diagnostic and therapeutic devices. (2)
      There is good ground to regard exams as
      initiation rites perhaps more cruel than
      breaking the candidates' teeth.
    Conclusion: No matter what courts decide about
      separation of church and state, there will
      be prayers in our schools as long as we
      have exams.

13

6. First Argument:
       Premiss: As newcomers to the establishment,
           women are not jaded by corrupt precedent
           nor lulled into dreary acceptance of the
           status quo.
       Conclusion: Women are anxious to take on City
           Hall, to challenge the worst aspects of male
           authority--the corruption, the deceit, the
           arrogance--and to assert their own authority.
   Second argument:
       Premiss: The preceding conclusion.
       Conclusion: Once women begin actively to seek
           power, to seize the offensive, they will be
           formidable opponents.

7. Argument:
       Premisses: (1) The Constitution precludes the
           indictment of an incumbent President. (2)
           If the President could not be indicted, the
           lawyers reasoned, he could not be called
           before a grand jury.
       Conclusion: The President cannot be called before
           a grand jury.

8. Argument:
       Premiss: If [physicians, nurses, dentists, and
           dental technicians] each cost the patient
           roughly the same (if one could for the same
           price have the services of a better qualified
           person) no one would want to use a nurse or
           dental technician, even in small matters.
       Conclusion: ...on the question of wage or salary
           differentials, there may be good market
           reasons for insisting that the wages of a
           physician and dentist be greater than those
           of a nurse or dental technician.

9. First argument:
       Premiss: Some human rights on the scale con-
           structed by the "majority" opinion were
           fundamental to human liberty.
       Conclusion: Those human rights regarded as
           fundamental to human liberty were protected.
   Second argument:
       Premiss: Some human rights on the "majority"
           opinion scale were not fundamental to human
           liberty.
       Conclusion: Those human rights regarded as not
           fundamental to human liberty were not
           protected.
   Third argument:
       Premiss: The right of a public high school student
           to wear his or her hair as he or she might

14

choose was not considered a fundamental right.
Conclusion: That right of a public high school
student was therefore not afforded consti-
tutional protection.
11. Argument:
Premisses: (1) The first sentence in the passage.
(2) The second sentence in the passage. (3)
That part of the third sentence in the passage which precedes the semicolon.
Conclusion: Nurture, not nature, is our guide (to
masculine or feminine behavior.)
12. Argument:
Premisses: (1) Bohr's theory, and subsequent
refinements of it, could not make real pre-
dictions about the relative degree of bright-
ness of the lines in an atomic spectrum. (2)
Bohr's theory failed for neutral helium, in
which two electrons are present.
Conclusion: It became increasingly clear that
Bohr's theory was not complete.
13. Argument:
Premisses: The second, third, and fourth sentences
of the passage.
Conclusion: The first sentence of the passage.
14. Not an argument but a conditional statement.
16. Alternative interpretations are acceptable here. The
passage <u>can</u> be regarded as a series of
assertions rather than an argument. Or it
can be analysed as an
Argument:
Premiss: The first sentence of the passage.
Conclusion: The proposal that women be injected
into the combat role in war is an extreme
suggestion that exceeds the bounds of reason
and logic.
17. Not an argument but a proposed explanation of why the
Supreme Court ruled in 1954 against segrega-
tion in public schools.
18. Argument:
Premisses: (1) He whom evil is to befal must
in his own person exist at the very time
it comes, if the misery and suffering are
haply to have any place at all. (2) Death
precludes [a person's existing] and forbids
him to be, upon whom the ills can be brought.
Conclusion: You may be sure that we have nothing
to fear after death, and that he who exists
not, cannot become miserable.
19. Not an argument: the first sentence is a complex conditional statement, and the second a brief

15

comment about the matter.

21. First argument: (this is <u>reported</u> in the first
    sentence of the passage)
   Premiss: Most women are married.
   Conclusion: We in the Movement should not attack
    marriage.
  Second argument: (this is <u>mentioned</u> in the second
    sentence of the passage)
   Premiss: All women are oppressed.
   Conclusion: We should not come out against
    oppression.
  Third argument:
   Premisses: (1) The second argument above is not
    logical. (2) The first argument above is
    analogous to (like) the second argument.
   Conclusion: The first argument above is not
    logical.
  Fourth argument:
   Premisses: (1) Of all the oppressive institutions,
    marriage is the one that affects the most
    women. (2) The conclusion of the third
    argument above.
   Conclusion: If we are interested in building a
    mass movement of women, we should begin
    by attacking marriage.

22. First argument:
   Premiss: The scale of the expedition which
    Xerxes led to Greece in 480 shows that it
    was not a punitive operation, intended
    merely to inflict damage.
   Conclusion: The aim of Xerxes' expedition was
    conquest.
  Second argument:
   Premisses: (1) Herodotus's explanation for the
    Persian attack on European Greece is that
    minor incidents on the Greek fringe of the
    Persian Empire grew, until the king lost
    patience and decided to terminate them with
    a large expedition. (2) The preceding
    conclusion.
   Conclusion: Herodotus's explanation is not
    satisfactory.

23. Not an argument but a complicated conditional statement.

24. Argument:
   Premiss: When a projector attempts to establish
    a new manufacture, he must at first entice
    his workmen from other employments by higher
    wages than they can earn either in their own
    trades, or than the nature of his work would
    otherwise require, and a considerable time

must pass away before he can venture to
reduce them to the common level.
Conclusion: Where all other circumstances are
equal, wages are generally higher in new
than in old trades.
25. No arguments present; what we have here are explanations.
26. Not an argument but a complicated conditional statement.
27. No arguments present; what we have are explanations.
28. Argument:
Premiss: There is no way of knowing (from outside) when a tap is open.
Conclusion: It is impossible (for a mayor, or
the government) to order a tap closed.
29. First argument:
Premiss: A woman's work (housework) has the
lowliest status of almost any work in society.
Conclusion: A woman's work--housework--cannot
give her status.
Second argument:
Premiss: The preceding conclusion.
Conclusion: A woman must acquire her status
vicariously through her husband's work.
30. Argument:
Premisses: (1) Under the circumstances des-
cribed, a frog could kick a man completely
away from the ball of gold. (2) Men are not
usually so easily diverted from gold.
Conclusion: We may conclude, in the manner of
Aesop, that the force of avarice greatly
exceeds that of gravitation.
Exercises on pages 35-41
2. Inductive argument:
Premisses: (1) Hamilton was at no time a rich
man. (2) At his death Hamilton left a small
estate.
Conclusion: That Hamilton ever held any considerable sum in securities seems highly
improbable.
Only probability is claimed for the conclusion--
hence the argument is inductive rather than
deductive. That only probability is claimed
for the conclusion suggests that the first
premiss must be interpreted as stating either
that Hamilton at no time had much _money_ or
that Hamilton at no time lived like a rich
man. For if "he was at no time a rich man"
is taken literally, it would follow deductively that he never held any considerable
sum in securities.

17

3. Inductive argument:
      Premiss: From the protozoa to man there is no-
            where a very wide gap either in structure or
            in behavior.
      Conclusion: [From the protozoa to man] there is
            also nowhere a very wide mental gap.
      Only probability is claimed for the conclusion,
            which follows largely by analogy from the
            premiss (see Chapter 11).
4. Deductive argument:
      Premiss: We find it self-evident that women are
            a colonized group who have never--anywhere--
            been allowed self-determination.
      Conclusion: Therefore, all women who fight against
            their own oppression (colonized status) as
            females under male domination are anti-
            imperialist by definition.
      This argument is claimed to be very strongly
            deductive: its premiss is said to be "self-
            evident", its conclusion is said to follow
            "by definition."
6. First inductive argument:
      Premiss: (1) At an underprivileged school in
            Harlem, they used to test the intelligence
            of all the children at two-year intervals.
            (2) They found that every two years each
            advancing class came out ten points lower
            in "native intelligence."
      Conclusion: The combined efforts of home in-
            fluencing and school education, a powerful
            combination, succeeded in making the children
            significantly stupider year by year.
   Second inductive argument:
      Premiss: The preceding conclusion.
      Conclusion: If they had a few more years of com-
            pulsory home ties and compulsory education,
            all would end up as gibbering idiots.
      The first argument is from data to the alleged
            cause, hence inductive. The second argument
            is from the alleged cause to what would
            happen if it were allowed to operate over
            a longer period of time. This is called
            "extrapolation" and is inductive.
7. Deductive argument:
      Premiss: The Planets are seen at varying distances
            from the Earth.
      Conclusion: The centre of Earth is surely not the
            centre of their orbits.
8. Inductive argument:
      Premisses: (1) Man shares a considerable degree
            of genetic potential with apes and monkeys.
18

    (2) Anthropoid primates have been very
conservative species which have departed
little from the ancestral pattern of pri-
mate structure.
  Conclusion: It is quite reasonable to assume
    that studies of ape and monkey behavior
    can provide indirect evidence for the im-
    pact of evolution on man's behavior.

9. Deductive argument:
    Premiss: Humans are not non-humans.
    Conclusion: There are no grounds to assume that
     anything primates do is necessary, natural
     or desirable in humans.
  Inductive argument: (this is _reported_ in the second
    and third sentences of the passage)
    Premiss: It is found that male chimpanzees placed
     alone with infants will not "mother" them.
    Conclusion: (Jumping from hard data to ideolo-
     gical speculation, researchers conclude
     from this information that) _human_ females
     are necessary for the safe growth of human
     infants.
  Inductive argument: (this is _mentioned_ in the last
    sentence of the passage)
    Premiss: [Teaching the young to speak] has been
     tried with chimpanzees and it does not work.
    Conclusion: It is quite useless to (try to)
     teach human infants to speak.
  Inductive argument: (not quite explicitly formulated
    in the passage)
    Premisses: (1) The second inductive argument
     above is illogical. (2) The first and second
     inductive arguments above are equally
     reasonable or logical.
    Conclusion: The first inductive argument above
     is illogical.

11. Deductive argument:
    Premisses: (1) You cannot have a rational
     justification for your appeal to history till
     your metaphysics has assured you that there
     _is_ a history to appeal to. (2) Your con-
     jectures as to the future presuppose some
     basis of knowledge that there _is_ a future
     already subjected to some determination.
    Conclusion: Induction presupposes metaphysics.
     In other words, it rests upon an antecedent
     rationalism.

12. Inductive argument:
    Premisses: (1) In Egypt food is constantly
     supplied to captive animals and as a con-

sequence the very fiercest creatures live
peaceably together. (2) In Egypt the very
fiercest creatures are tamed by kindness,
and in some places crocodiles are tame to
their priestly keepers from being fed by
them. (3) Elsewhere the same phenomenon is
to be observed.

Conclusion: If there were no lack or stint of
food, then those animals that are now afraid
of people or are wild by nature would be
tame and familiar with them and in like
manner with one another.

The premisses of this argument (which have themselves been inductively established) assert
that certain causes have had certain effects
in this or that particular locality. The
conclusion generalizes, claiming that those
causes would have those effects generally.
This is an inductive generalization, another
extrapolation, and so is inductive.

13. Deductive argument:

Premiss: The family structure is the <u>source</u> of
psychological, economic, and political
oppression.

Conclusion: Any initial liberation under current
socialism must always revert back to re-
pression.

Deductive argument:

Premiss: Socialist attempts to soften the structure of power within the family by incor-
porating women into the labor force or army
are only reformist.

Conclusion: Socialism as it is now constituted
in the various parts of the world is not
only no improvement on capitalism, but often
worse.

14. Deductive argument:

Premisses: (1) Far more than any other system,
the market through competition fosters
technical innovation and provides for the
replacement of obsolete products and modes
of production--[which] perhaps more than
anything else, makes market systems produc-
tive. (2) Central planning, by contrast,
inhibits the introduction of the new and
the replacement of the obsolete--which helps
account for its relatively low productivity.

Conclusion: The market is so efficient that even
if only a small percentage of the national
income is redistributed, more is available

20

for redistribution to those disadvantaged
by nature or misfortune than in alternative
systems.
Inductive argument:
Premiss: The preceding conclusion.
Conclusion: Although its distributional in-
equalities may lack moral justification, the
market system is likely to lead to superior
economic results for everyone.

16. Deductive argument:
Premiss: [When they propose to establish the
universal from the particulars by means of
induction] if they review some of the particular instances, some of the particulars
omitted in the induction may contravene the
universal.
Conclusion: [When they propose to establish the
universal from the particulars by means of
induction] if they review some of the particular instances, the induction will be
insecure.
Deductive argument:
Premiss: Particulars are infinite and indefinite.
Conclusion: [When they propose to establish the
universals from the particulars by means of
induction] if they are to review all [of the
particular instances], they will be toiling
at the impossible.
Deductive argument:
Premisses: (1) When they propose to establish
the universal from the particulars by means
of induction, they will effect this by a
review either of all or of some of the particular instances. (2) The conjunction of
the two preceding conclusions.
Conclusion: Induction is invalidated and the
method of induction is easy to set aside.
Although these arguments are about induction they
are themselves deductive.

17. Deductive argument.
The first two sentences express the premisses
and the last sentence the conclusion. Although the premisses may themselves have
been established inductively, the conclusion
is inferred from them not as just likely or
probably, but the strong claim is made that
the things we are talking about when we
describe our sensations "cannot" be processes in the brain.

18. Inductive argument:

21

Premisses: (1) If we found by chance a watch or
other piece of intricate mechanism we should
infer that it had been made by someone. (2)
All around us we do find intricate pieces
of natural mechanism, and the processes of
the universe are seen to move together
in complex relations.
Conclusion: We should infer that these two have
a Maker. /This conclusion follows only by
analogy from the premisses, and the argument is therefore inductive (see Chapter 11)./

19. Inductive argument:
Premiss: Love, perhaps even more than child-
bearing, is the pivot of women's oppression
today.
Conclusion: A book on radical feminism that did
not deal with love would be a political
failure.
This argument is inductive if the writer is using
the word "political" in the customary sense
in which a political act (or book) is a
political failure if it does not lead to the
end aimed at. For here the writer would be
appealing to the empirical fact--if it is a
fact--that political acts usually fail if
they do not pay attention to the essence of
the problem addressed. However, if the word
is used in the more philosophical sense in
which a political act (or book) is a failure
simply if it misses the central political
point, i.e. does not focus squarely on what
is the fulcrom or pivot of the political
situation addressed, then the argument is
deductive rather than inductive.

21. Deductive argument:
Premiss: There are more people on earth than hairs
on any one person's head.   ,
Conclusion: There must be at least two people with
the same number of hairs.
The premiss must be arrived at inductively (statis-
tically) but the conclusion follows from it
deductively.

22. Deductive arguments:
(1) Premiss: Neither peace of mind for the present
nor intelligent planning for the future is
possible for men who either live without rules
or cannot abide by the rules they have.
Conclusion: The life of every civilized community
is governed by rules.
(2) Premisses: (1) The preceding conclusion: (2)
Making rules for the community, and enforcing

them, is the job of government.

Conclusion: No community can be truly civilized
without an effective and reasonably stable
government.

Both these arguments seem to me to be enthymematic
(See Section 7.4). The suppressed premiss in
the first argument is: peace of mind for the
present and intelligent planning for the
future are essential for men to constitute a
civilized community. And the suppressed
premiss for the second argument is: no
government can make rules and enforce them
unless it is effective and reasonably stable.

23. Deductive argument.

The conclusion is stated in the first sentence,
the premisses in the second sentence.

24. Inductive argument.

Premiss: The three classes of modern society,
the feudal aristocracy, the bourgeoisie and
the proletariat, each have their special
morality.

Conclusion: Men consciously or unconsciously,
derive their moral ideas in the last resort
from the practical relations on which their
class position is based--from the economic
relations in which they carry on production
and exchange.

There are clearly two inductive leaps here: one
is from just three classes in one period to
all men at all times; the other from an
(alleged) regularity to a claimed causal
connection. (See Chapter 12)

25. Deductive argument:

Although the premiss of this argument, that it
took at least 2.3 seconds to operate the bolt
action on Oswald's rifle, was established
inductively by tests, the present argument
simply assumes that as a premiss from which
its own conclusion is claimed to follow
necessarily.

Premisses: (1) It took at least 2.3 seconds to
operate the bolt action on Oswald's rifle.
(2) In the time it takes to fire 3 shots it
is only necessary to operate the bolt twice.

Conclusion: Oswald definitely could fire 3 shots
in less than 5.6 seconds.

26. Inductive argument:

Premisses: (1) In all my small experience with
guns I had never hit anything I had tried
to hit. (2) I had tried to hit that man.

23

Conclusion: I had not touched (hit) that man.
The experience referred to is _previous_ experience,
and the conclusion concerning the present
case is claimed to follow only by "the law
or probabilities."

27. Deductive argument:
Premisses: (1) Women high school students are of
smaller size than men high school students.
(2) Women high school students have had
less athletic training than men high school
students.
Conclusion: In a high school of 2,000 students,
which had 10 athletic teams limited to 20
persons each, it is obvious that women students would be effectively precluded from
participating in the state-sponsored athletic
program of that school.
Deductive argument:
Premiss: The preceding conclusion.
Conclusion: Such a school rule (as required by
the E.R.A.), although sex-neutral by its
terms, would in fact discriminate against
the right of women students to participate
in high school athletics on an equal basis
with men.

28. Inductive argument: The four premisses are neatly
numbered in the whole of the passage past
the colon. The conclusion that Mitchell
and Colson were conspirators is said to be
"inescapable," but it is obvious that only
inductive evidence is offered for it.

29. Inductive argument: The three premisses are stated
in the first, second, and fourth sentences
of the passage. The conclusion is stated
in the third sentence. The inference is
surely "irresistible" psychologically, but
it is of course logically possible that
sheer and unlikely coincidence could account
for messages "identical even down to commas
and semicolons."

30. Deductive argument:
Premisses: (1) The Lord says _It repenteth Me_
that I have made man.
(2) Whoever repents of what he has done,
has a changeable will.
Conclusion: Therefore God has a changeable will.

31. Deductive argument:
The first sentence contains and premiss (or
premisses) and the second sentence contains
the (compound) conclusion. No evidence or

24

data is offered to show that people
cannot understand things unless they understand the things' contexts, and cannot say
what things are unless they can say what
the things' contexts are. Collingwood
seems to think this is known independently
of any evidence. His phrase "I venture
to infer" may suggest that probable inference rather than demonstration was intended, but to me it looks more like pre-
ciosity.

32. Inductive argument:
Premisses: (1) Over the last quarter-century,
as this is written, the average work week
in industry has increased moderately. (2)
During this period average weekly earnings,
adjusted for price increases, have nearly
doubled.
Conclusion: As their incomes rise, men will work
longer hours and seek less leisure.
The conclusion is a generalization from a re-
stricted sample: from what was true for
a 25 year period to an (alleged) general
tendency.

Exercises on pages 44-48
2. First argument:
Premiss: Mankind always act in order to obtain
that which they think good.
Conclusion: Every community is established with
a view to some good.
Second argument:
Premisses: (1) Every community is established
with a view to some good.
(2) The state is a political community which
is highest of all and which embraces all
other communities.
(3) If all communities aim at some good then
the state aims at good in a greater degree
than any other and at the highest good.
(Perhaps this premiss does not have to be
stated explicitly.)
Conclusion: The state aims at good in a greater
degree than any other and at the highest
good.
3. First argument:
Premiss: One reason why it's so difficult for
low-skilled people to find employment is
because the Social Security tax raises the
employer's cost of hiring them.
25

Conclusion: The Social Security tax discourages
the employment of people.

Second argument:
Premisses: (1) The Social Security system rests
on a payroll tax, which is a regressive
tax imposing a heavy burden on the lowest
income groups. (2) The preceding conclusion.
Conclusion: The Social Security tax system is a
bad tax system.

Third argument:
Premisses: (1) Under the Social Security benefit
system, a man who gets a million dollars a
year from property receives his full Social
Security so-called benefits when he retires.
(2) A person who continues to work and earns
more than a limited sum does not receive a
penny from Social Security between ages 65
to 72 and continues to pay the tax!
Conclusion: The Social Security system is a very
bad welfare system (which is silly and makes
no sense.)

Fourth argument:
Premisses: (1) The conclusion of the second argument. (2) The conclusion of the third argument.
Conclusion: What Social Security really is is a
combination of a very poor tax system and a
very bad welfare program.

Fifth argument:
Premisses: (1) The Social Security system, as it
is now, is presented as if it were an insurance scheme, whereby individuals are pay-
ing their own money to provide their own
retirement. (2) The preceding conclusion.
Conclusion: The Social Security system, as it
is now, is a farce and a fraud.

4. Mainly this passage offers an explanation of why
"women often refuse to argue logically."
But two arguments can be discerned within it.

First argument:
Premisses: (1) Male logic can only deal with
simple issues. (2) Women, because they are
passive and condemned to observe and react
rather than initiate, are more aware of
complexity.
Conclusion: Men are not rational animals.

Second argument:
Premisses: (1) Arguments between women and their
menfolk are disguised realpolitik. (2) Such
an argument is not a contest of mental
agility with the right as the victor's

26

spoils, but a contest of wills. (3) In such
arguments the rules of logical discourse are
no more relevant than the Marquess of Queens-
berry's are to a pub brawl. (4) The preceding conclusion.

Conclusion: In most situations logic is simply
rationalization of an infralogical aim.

6. First argument:

Premisses: (1) All that we perceive by sense are
our own ideas or sensations.
(2) Houses, mountains, rivers, and in a word
all sensible objects, are things we perceive
by sense.

Conclusion: Houses, mountains, etc., are our own
ideas or sensations.

Second argument:

Premisses: (1) The preceding conclusion.
(2) None of our own ideas or sensations can
exist unperceived.

Conclusion: Houses, mountains, etc., cannot exist
unperceived.

Third argument:

Premiss: The immediately preceding conclusion.

Conclusion: That houses, mountains, etc., have
an existence, natural or real, distinct
from their being perceived by the understanding, involves a manifest contradiction.

7. First argument:

Premiss: By international law the closing of the
Gulf of Akaba (in 1967) constituted a casus
belli (a cause of war), as Nasser himself had
acknowledged.

Conclusion: Israel was not the aggressor.

Second argument:

Premiss: There was no mother-country.

Conclusion: Israel did not carry off raw materials
and send them back to a mother-country that
would sell the manufactured products to the
colonies at a high price.

Third argument:

Premisses: (1) Israel did not exploit a native
labour-force. (2) The preceding conclusion.

Conclusion: Israel was not colonialist.

Fourth argument:

Premisses: (1) The Americans had no base in
Israel. (2) Americans drew no wealth from
Israel. (3) Although Americans did have
military bases in the Arab states, did exploit Arab oil, and did provide the Arabs
with important economic aid.

27

Conclusion: Israel is no bridgehead for im-
perialism.
Fifth argument:
Premisses: (1) Israel did not prevent Algeria
from winning its independence. (2) Israel
did not prevent Nasser from building the
Aswan dam. (3) Israel did not prevent Libya
from successfully carrying out its revolution.
Conclusion: It is not true that Israel's existence hindered the development of the Arab
countries.
Sixth argument:
Premiss: The only factor that these (Arab) states,
strangers to one another or even enemies,
have in common is their hatred for Israel.
Conclusion: The existence of Israel is the very
reason why unity of the Arab world is at
least to some degree achieved.
Seventh argument:
Premiss: The preceding conclusion.
Conclusion: The existence of Israel is not an
impediment to the unity of the Arab world.
8. First argument:
Premiss: Music, for example, is good to a
melancholy person, bad to one mourning,
while to a deaf man it is neither good nor
bad.
Conclusion: One and the same thing may at the
same time be both good and evil or indifferent.
Second argument:
Premiss: One and the same thing may at the same
time be both good and evil or indifferent.
Conclusion: With regard to good and evil,...of
one thing with another.
9. First argument:
Premisses: (1) Of the voluntary acts of every
man, the object is some good to himself.
(2) A man's transference or renunciation of
his right is a voluntary act.
Conclusion: Whensoever a man transferreth his
right, or renounceth it; it is either in
consideration of some right reciprocally
transferred to himself, or for some other
good he hopeth for thereby.
Second argument:
Premisses: (1) The preceding conclusion.
(2) A man cannot be understood to aim at any
good to himself by laying down the right of
28

                resisting them that assault him by force,
                to take away his life.
           Conclusion: A man cannot lay down the right of
                resisting them that assault him by force,
                to take away his life.
      Third argument:
           Premiss: The immediately preceding conclusion.
           Conclusion: There be some rights which no man
                can be understood by any words, or other
                signs, to have abandoned or transferred.
11.   Premisses: (1) All <u>talents</u> of the mind (intelligence,
           wit, etc.) may be put to bad use.
           (2) All <u>gifts</u> <u>of</u> <u>fortune</u> (power, riches, etc.)
           may be put to bad use.
           Conclusion: Nothing can possibly be conceived
                in the world, or even out of it, which can
                be called good without qualification, except
                a <u>good</u> <u>will</u>.
12.   First argument:
           Premiss: The object of reasoning...which we do
                not know.
           Conclusion: Reasoning is good if...and not
                otherwise.
      Second argument:
           Premiss: The preceding conclusion.
           Conclusion: The question of its validity...and
                not of thinking.
      Third argument:
           Premiss: The immediately preceding conclusion.
           Conclusion: A being the premisses...accept the
                conclusion also.
      Fourth argument:
           Premisses: (1) The immediately preceding con-
                clusion.
                (2) It is true that we do generally reason
                correctly by nature.
           Conclusion: But that is an accident...tendency
                to believe in it.
13.   First argument:
           Premiss: The bulk of mankind are certain to
                commit fallacies.
           Conclusion: Ordinary men and women should be
                taught logic, so as to be able to refrain
                from drawing conclusions which only <u>seem</u>
                to follow.
      Second argument:
           Premisses: (1) Logic was, formerly, the art of
                drawing inferences.
                (2) It has appeared that the inferences we
                naturally feel inclined to make are hardly
                                29

        ever valid.
    Conclusion: Logic has now become the art of
    abstaining from inference.
Third argument:
    Premisses: (1) If people reason, they will almost
    certainly reason wrongly.
    (2) Reasoning wrongly (as do the French) is
    a most undesirable quality.
    (3) Logic has now become the art of abstain-
    ing from inferences (the immediately pre-
    ceding conclusion).
    Conclusion: Logic ought to be taught in schools
    with a view to teaching people not to reason.
Exercises on pages 49-54
    2. The blind man must have on a white hat, for if he had
        on a red hat, one of the other prisoners would have
        known the color of the hat on his own head. If one
        of the other prisoners as well as the blind man had
        a red hat, the other one, seeing two red hats would
        know the color of his own hat to be white and would
        have said so. If both the other prisoners had white
        hats then the second to reply would have known that
        his hat was white, since if it were red as well as the
        blind man's, the first would have known his own hat
        to be white, which he did not.
    3. Mr. Jones is not the brakeman's next-door neighbor,
        for if he were his earnings would be divisible by 3(e),
        but he earns exactly $20,000/year (c) and that sum is
        not divisible by 3. Mr. Robinson is not the brakeman's
        next-door neighbor, for if he were he would live
        halfway between Detroit and Chicago (b), but he lives
        in Detroit (a). Hence, Mr. Smith is the brakeman's
        next-door neighbor.
        Neither Mr. Robinson (a) nor Mr. Smith (by the above
        argument) lives in Chicago. Hence, Mr. Jones lives
        in Chicago and so Jones is the brakeman (f).
        Smith is not the fireman (d) and Jones is not the
        fireman (by the above argument).
        Hence, Robinson is the fireman, and the engineer's
        name is Smith.
    4. The manager has a grandson and is, therefore, not
        Mr. Black, the bachelor, nor the 22-year old Mr. White,
        nor Miss Ambrose, nor Miss Earnshaw, who are un-
        married, nor Mr. Kelly, who is the manager's neighbor.
        Therefore, the manager is Mrs. Coffee.
        The stenographer has a married child and is, therefore,
        not Mr. Black, Miss Ambrose, nor Miss Earnshaw, who
        are unmarried, nor the 22-year old Mr. White, nor Mrs.
        Coffee the manager. Therefore, Mr. Kelly is the
        stenographer. The cashier is a married man since he

is a son-in-law, and is, therefore, neither Mr. Black,
the bachelor, nor any of the females, Mrs. Coffee,
Miss Ambrose, nor Miss Earnshaw, nor is he Mr. Kelly,
the stenographer.
Therefore, Mr. White is the cashier.
The assistant manager is a grandson, and, therefore,
is none of the females, nor by the above is he Mr. Kelly
nor Mr. White. Therefore, Mr. Black is the assistant
manager. The teller is not her own step-sister and so
is not Miss Ambrose. Nor is she any of the above
identified persons: Mrs. Coffee, Mr. Kelly, Mr. White,
or Mr. Black. Therefore, the teller is Miss Earnshaw.
Finally, by elimination, Miss Ambrose is the clerk.

6. Since Ms. Adams stayed on the main floor where books
are sold, Ms. Adams bought a book.
Seven people entered the elevator, Ms. Fisk was the
seventh to leave it and Ms. Ennis was the sixth person
to leave it, getting off at the fifth floor and buying
a lamp. (Ms. Ennis bought a lamp). The two women who
got off at the second floor bought a necktie and a
handbag. Ms. Catt did not buy a necktie, so Ms. Catt
bought a handbag.
Ms. Fisk bought neither a book (1st floor), a dress
(3rd floor), a necktie (2nd floor), a handbag (2nd
floor), nor a lamp (5th floor). Therefore, Ms. Fisk
bought a hat. Ms. Baker bought neither book, lamp,
handbag, nor hat, by the above arguments. Nor did she
buy a necktie, since one of the other women bought it
and gave it to Mr. Baker.
Therefore, Ms. Baker bought a dress. And so Ms. Dodge
bought the necktie.

7. White does not live in Brownsville, nor does Nash, nor
does Brown, nor does Harper. Therefore, Peters lives
in Brownsville. Brown is not a barber, nor is Nash,
nor is Peters (by the above), nor is Harper. Therefore,
White is a barber.
Harper is not a barber, nor a writer, nor a heating
contractor, nor a neurologist (since he lives in
Nashville). Therefore, Harper is a printer.
Nash is neither barber, nor heating contractor, nor
a neurologist, nor a printer. Therefore, Nash is a
writer.
Brown is neither heating contractor, nor printer, nor
barber, nor writer. Therefore, Brown is a neurologist.
Hence, Peters is the heating contractor.
Brown lives in neither Petersburg, nor Harper's Ferry,
nor in Brownsville, nor in Nashville (since Harper
lives there).
Therefore, Brown lives in White Plains. White is not a

resident of Brownsville, nor of White Plains, nor of
Nashville, nor of Petersburg (being the barber).
Therefore, White lives in Harper's Ferry.
Nash does not live in Brownsville, nor in Nashville,
nor in either White Plains or Harper's Ferry. There-
fore, Nash lives in Petersburg.

8. Since Otto accused The Kid, The Kid's first and fourth
statements are equivalent and, therefore, either both
true or both false. Since only one of his statements
can be false, they are both true. Therefore, Otto's
third statement is false and the rest are true. His
fourth statement being true entails that Mickey's
third statement is false, and so Mickey's other statements are true. The truth of Mickey's fourth statement entails that Curly's fourth statement is true.
The truth of Mickey's second statement entails that
The Kid's second statement is true, and hence The Kid's
third statement is false, from which it follows that
Curly's third statement is true. The truth of Otto's
first statement entails that Slim's third statement
is true. The statement of the problem shows that
Slim's second and fourth statements are true also, so
Slim's first statement must be false, from which it
follows that Curly's second statement is true. Since
Curly's fourth and third statements have already been
shown to be true above, his first statement must be
the false one. Hence Curly dunnit.

9. (The argument here is easy to go through with a diagram,
difficult without one.)

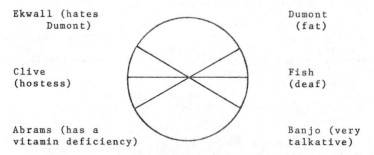

Ekwall (hates Dumont)

Dumont (fat)

Clive (hostess)

Fish (deaf)

Abrams (has a vitamin deficiency)

Banjo (very talkative)

11. Notice that there are six men, three married women, and
two unmarried women. The following are men: the Third
VP (a), the First VP (f), the Cashier (f), the Janitor
(g), and the Teller (j). That makes five men, so there

is only one other man. The Second VP and the Assistant
Teller are of the same sex (c), and thus both women,
so the Bookkeeper is the sixth man (i). Thus, the other
women are the President, the First Stenographer and the
Second Stenographer. The sex of each person as estab-
lished above will be referred to as (1). The President
is a woman (1) and married (a) and so is either Mrs.
Brown, Mrs. Ford, or Mrs. Kane, but she is not Mrs.
Brown (a), nor Mrs. Kane (e), so the President is Mrs.
Ford (m).
The Second Stenographer is a woman (1) and unmarried
(h) and so is either Miss Dale or Miss Hill, but she
is not Miss Hill (d), so the Second Stenographer is
Miss Dale (n).
The Assistant Teller is a woman (1) and married (b)
[otherwise she would have the same last name as her
unmarried sister (h)], but she is not Mrs. Ford (m),
nor Mrs. Brown (a), so the Assistant Teller is Mrs.
Kane (o).
The First Stenographer is a woman (1) and married (j),
but she is not Mrs. Ford (m), nor Mrs. Kane (o), so
the First Stenographer is Mrs. Brown (p).
The second VP is a woman (1), but she is not Mrs. Ford
(m), nor Miss Dale (n), nor Mrs. Kane (o), nor Mrs.
Brown (p), so the Second VP is Miss Hill (q).
Mr. Grant is either the President or the First VP (d
and q), but he is not the President (m), so the First
VP is Mr. Grant (r). Mr. Grant lives at the Bachelor's
Club (f and r), so the Cashier is one of the President's nearest neighbors (f and e), and so the cashier
is either Mrs. Kane or Mr. Long, but the Cashier is
not Mrs. Kane (o), so the Cashier is Mr. Long (s).
The Bookkeeper is a man (1), but he is not Mr. Evans
(k), nor Mr. Jones (k), nor Mr. Adams (h and k), nor
Mr. Grant (r), nor Mr. Long (s), so the Bookkeeper is
Mr. Camp (t).
The Teller is a man (1), but he is not Mr. Grant (r),
nor Mr. Long (s), nor Mr. Camp (t), nor Mr. Adams
(h and k), nor Mr. Evans (j and k), so the Teller is
Mr. Jones (u).
The Third VP is a man (1), but he is not Mr. Grant
(r), nor Mr. Long (s), nor Mr. Camp (t), nor Mr.
Jones (u), nor Mr. Evans (a and k), so the Third VP
is Mr. Adams (v).
And by elimination, the Janitor is Mr. Evans.
12. Jones had Luckies, because Perkins did not (by e),
Reilly did not (by b and d), Turner did not (by b
and d), and Brown did not because he originally had
only 3 cigarettes (by f) and one man had smoked 5

cigarettes (by d) and the Luckies smoker had smoked
at least 2 more than anyone else (by e). The Chesterfield smoker (by c) either originally had 15 cigarettes
and had smoked 10 or else originally had 20 cigarettes
and had smoked 13. But if the latter, then the Luckies
smoker must have smoked at least 15, but must have had
originally only 15 and, therefore, must have smoked
all his cigarettes contrary to condition g. So the
Chesterfield smoker must have originally had 15 cigarettes of which he smoked 10. Jones originally had
20 Luckies, because the Luckies smoker must have smoked
at least 12, to do which he must have had over 8
originally, and he could not have had 15 since the
Chesterfield smoker had 15.
Since Reilly smoked half of his original supply (by
b) he must have originally had an even number of cigarettes, other than 20 (Jones had the 20). Therefore,
he originally had either 8 or 6 and has smoked either
4 or 3. So Turner must have smoked either 5 or 4.
Hence neither Reilly nor Turner smoked Chesterfields.
Turner must have smoked Kools, because Jones did not
(he smoked Luckies), Perkins did not (he asked for 3
cards and the Kool smoker drew to an inside straight--
only Kools of the 5 brands mentioned are mentholated),
Brown did not (he drew 3 aces whereas the Kool smoker
drew to an inside straight), and Reilly did not, since
he smoked either 4 or 3 whereas the Kool smoker has
smoked 5 cigarettes.
Turner smoked 5 Kools (by d), so Reilly must have
smoked 4 (by b) and, therefore, Reilly originally had
8 cigarettes. Brown originally had 3 cigarettes (f),
Reilly had 8, Jones had 20, the Chesterfield smoker
had 15, so Turner originally had 6 Kools.
Perkins originally had 15 Chesterfields, since the other
numbers were had by the other men and only the Chesterfields originally totaled 15.
Either Reilly or Brown smoked Camels, but it was not
Brown (by h), so it must have been Reilly. Therefore,
Reilly originally had 8 Camels.
And so Brown originally had 3 Old Golds.

13.   The pilot did not wear pink or blue (because she often
         played bridge with the women in pink and blue)
         and did not wear white (because the housewife
         wore white). Therefore the pilot wore yellow.
      Carol was not the pilot, nor did Carol wear pink or
         blue (because Carol and the pilot often played
         bridge with the women in pink and blue). Carol
         did not wear yellow (Carol was not the pilot
         and the pilot wore yellow). So Carol wore white
         and was therefore the housewife.

The professor did not wear blue (she envied the woman
in blue). Neither did the professor wear white
(the housewife did) nor yellow (the pilot did).
So the professor wore pink.
Alice did not wear blue (she envied the woman in blue).
Nor did Alice wear pink (Alice and the professor
envied the woman in blue and the professor wore
pink). Nor did Alice wear white (since Carol
wore white). So Alice wore yellow and was therefore the pilot.
Betty was not the lifeguard (the lifeguard beat Betty
at Canasta), nor the pilot (who was Alice), nor
the housewife (who was Carol). Therefore Betty
was the professor and wore pink.
Dorothy (by elimination) was the lifeguard and wore
blue.

14. For definiteness let us suppose that the traveler can
point to one branch and call it "R" (for the right
hand branch), and that he refers to the native
as "you". The traveler should ask:
Is it the case that R is the road to the
capital if and only if you are a politician?
Case 1. The native answers "yes".
Subcase 1. A. The native is a politician.
In this subcase the native's answer is
false, and so it is not the case that R
is the road to the capital if and only
if the native is a politician. But the
native is a politician, so R is not the
road to the capital.
Subcase 1. B. The native is not a politician. In this subcase the native's answer
is true, and so it is the case that R is
the road to the capital if and only if
the native is a politician. But the
native is not a politician, so R is not
the road to the capital.
So whether the native is a politician or
not, if he answers "yes" to this question,
R is not the road to the capital.
Case 2. The native answers "no".
Subcase 2. A. The native is a politician.
In this subcase the native's answer is
false, and it is the case that R is the
road to the capital if and only if the
native is a politician. The native is a
politician so R is the road to the
capital.
Subcase 2. B. The native is not a politician.
In this subcase the native's answer is

true and it is not the case that R is the road
to the capital if and only if the native is a
politician. But the native is not a politician
so R is the road to the capital.

So whether the native is a politician or not, if he
answers "no" to this question, R is the road to
the capital.

An alternative method of solving this problem was
communicated to me by Professor Paul Mercken of
The Florida State University, who proposes that
the traveller should ask:

Would you say "yes" if I asked you whether
R is the road to the capital?

Case 1. The native answers "yes."

Subcase 1. A. The native is a politician. In this
subcase the native's answer is false, so he
would say "no" to the question whether R is
the road to the capital. But since the native
is a politician, he would speak falsely, whence
R is the road to the capital.

Subcase 1. B. The native is not a politician. In
this subcase the native's answer is true, so he
would say "yes" to the question whether R is the
road to the capital. Since the native is not a
politician, he would tell the truth, whence R is
the road to the capital.

Case 2. The native answers "no."

Subcase 2. A. The native is a politician. In this
subcase the native's answer is false, so he would
say "yes" to the question whether R is the road
to the capital. But since the native is a
politician, he would speak falsely, whence R
is not the road to the capital.

Subcase 2. B. The native is not a politician. In
this subcase the native's answer is true, so he
would say "no" to the question whether R is the
road to the capital. Since the native is not
a politician, he would tell the truth, whence R is
not the road to the capital.

So whether the native is a politician or not. if he
answers "yes" to this question, R is the road
to the capital.

Exercises on pages 65-70

I.   2. Directive: Let us learn how to rehabilitate criminals;
OR--Don't let questions about rehabilitation of
criminals into the legal issue of punishment for
crimes and the protection of society from
criminals.

Expressive: To evoke a desire to learn how to rehabilitate criminals; OR--To evoke a sterner

attitude towards criminals, who must be punished
and from whom society must be protected; OR--
to express exasperation with those who are concerned with rehabilitation of criminals rather
than with punishment, deterrence, and the protection of society.
Informative: (an argument) No one knows how to rehabilitate criminals, therefore judges do not know
how to rehabilitate criminals.

3. Directive: Let us honor and reward farmers and farming.
Expressive: To express and evoke respect and approbation for farmers and farming.
Informative: (an argument) When tillage begins, other
arts follow. Therefore farmers are the founders
of human civilization.

4. Directive: Let us do something about the evils that
threaten us.
Expressive: To evoke concern and energy about threat-
ening evils.
Informative: If good men combat evil, evil cannot
triumph.

6. Directive: Do not think only of pleasure.
Expressive: To evoke interest in things other than
pleasure.
Informative: Here is an argument intended to prove
that if only pleasure is sought then no pleasure
will be found.

7. Directive: Don't attempt to establish a uniform
equality of wages.
Expressive: To evoke an accepting attitude towards
wage differentials.
Informative: It is the bad workmen who believe in
the elimination of wage differentials.

8. Directive: Oppose war.
Expressive: To evoke an attitude of abhorrence for war.
Informative: War destroys religion, states, and
families. It is the greatest plague that can
afflict humanity, and any scourge is preferable
to it.

9. Directive: Support and extend education.
Expressive: To evoke approval of education.
Informative: If education is not strengthened and
furthered we shall suffer catastrophe.

11. Directive: Arm yourselves.
Expressive: To evoke feelings of antipathy towards
disarmament.
Informative: People despise those who are unarmed.

12. Directive: Make (or at least prepare for) war.
Expressive: To evoke feelings of antipathy toward
peace, and approbation of war.

37

Informative: Eternal peace is impossible; war develops the noblest virtues of man: courage and abnegation, dutifulness and self-sacrifice; and war protects the world from materialism.

13. Directive: Watch your language!
   Expressive: To evoke feelings of respect for language.
   Informative: Language is essential to mental life, embodying thoughts and necessary for the development of thought.

14. Directive: Do not oppose war.
   Expressive: To evoke approval of war.
   Informative: War at present has more good than bad consequences.

16. Directive: Work to eliminate patriotism.
   Expressive: To evoke antipathy towards patriotism.
   Informative: Patriotism is the basic cause of conflict.

17. Directive: Understand and acknowledge that there is a real difference between virtue and vice.
   Expressive: To evoke antipathy towards and distrust of the "ethical relativist."
   Informative: The "ethical relativist" is probably not to be trusted.

18. Directive: Practice eugenics.
   Expressive: To evoke disapproval of current casual marriage selection practice.
   Informative: People try to improve the breed in mating domestic animals, but take no such care in human mating.

19. Directive: Don't believe the Bible.
   Expressive: To evoke feelings of sceptical amusement at, rather than belief in, the Bible.
   Informative: It would have been more nearly miraculous for Jonah to have swallowed the whale than vice versa.

21. Informative: (an argument) If a person's desires were not directed toward a particular external thing itself, distinct from the pleasure arising from it, no pleasure could arise from it more than from another thing. Therefore all particular appetites and passions are toward external things themselves, distinct from the pleasure arising from them.

22. Directive: Do not marry Mr. Collins.
   Expressive: To evoke a feeling of distaste for Mr. Collins.
   ?Informative: (an argument) If you marry Mr. Collins I will never see you again and if you do not marry Mr. Collins your mother will never see you again; (therefore) from this day you must be a stranger

to one of your parents.

23. Expressive: To evoke feelings of disapproval toward
        Mr. Pickwick.
    ?Informative: Mr. Pickwick is a revoltingly heartless,
        systematic villain.
24. Expressive: To evoke feelings of disapproval toward
        "these elder statesmen."
    Directive: Do not praise "these elder statesmen."
    Informative: "These elder statesmen" have improved
        the city's material position but have caused its
        moral condition to deteriorate.
25. Directive: Avoid civil war, do not avoid foreign wars.
    Expressive: To evoke antipathy towards civil war
        and approval of foreign wars.
    Informative: Civil war weakens a nation; foreign wars
        strengthen a nation.
II. 2. Asserts that the government's classification of ice as
        a "food product" implies that Antarctica is one
        of the world's foremost food producers.
    Intended to cause rejection of government bureaus'
        rulings and classifications.
    Provides evidence that the speaker (writer) has a sharp
        wit and that he is opposed to (some) governmental
        intrusion into business.
3. Asserts that the proper function of criticism is to
        recommend good things, not to denounce bad ones.
    Intended to cause critics to report and recommend
        what is good rather than to spend any time de-
        nouncing what is bad.
    Provides evidence that the speaker is more interested
        in enjoying what is good rather than scorning
        what isn't.
4. Asserts two propositions, the first as premiss and the
        second as conclusion:
        (1) Earth without music is like an incomplete and
        unoccupied house.
        (2) Therefore the earliest history of every nation
        begins with music.
    Intended to cause people to take a greater interest in,
        and to have more respect for, music.
    Provides evidence that the speaker is high on music
        and weak in logic.
6. Asserts that the speaker has attempted not to respond
        emotionally to men's actions but to understand
        them.
    Intended to promote acceptance of the writer's explana-
        tions as "objective."
    Provides evidence that the writer is persuasive and
        is more interested in explaining than in mourning,
        condemning, or being entertained by human actions.

7. Asserts that political liberty is completely useless
      for the poor, and valuable only to ambitious
      theorists and politicians.
   Intended to diminish the esteem in which political
      liberty is held and to produce hostility to
      those who praise it.
   Provides evidence that the speaker is more interested
      in economic than in political libertarian issues.

8. Asserts that the speaker identifies with the lower,
      criminal, and imprisoned sections of society.
   Intended to cause a reappraisal of the worth of the
      lower classes.
   Provides evidence of the humanitarianism and the radical
      sentiments of the speaker.

9. Asserts that democracy is not a suitable form of
      government for men.
   Intended to diminish people's faith in the workability
      of democratic institutions.
   Provides evidence of the speaker's opposition to
      democratic institutions.

11. Asserts that turbulence and all other evil tempers of
      this evil age belong to the middle classes rather
      than to the lower classes.
   Intended to cause hostility toward the middle classes
      rather than toward the lower classes.
   Provides evidence that the speaker is hostile towards
      the middle classes, and not (or at least does not
      regard himself as) middle class himself.

12. Asserts that war will always recur, with (or as) God's
      blessing (!), and constitutes a drastic cure for
      what ails us.
   Intended to cause acceptance of war (as holy and help-
      ful) and to diminish opposition to it.
   Provides evidence that the speaker is pro-war, reli-
      gious, and persuaded that mankind is sick.

13. Asserts that the speaker would prefer to be qualified
      for but not possessed of the Presidency than
      possessed of but not qualified for the Presidency.
   Intended to recommend himself to the (Republican)
      party as candidate for President, and also to
      cast doubt on Abraham Lincoln's qualifications
      for the Presidency.
   Provides evidence that the speaker is not President
      and also that the speaker is conceited.

14. Asserts that Disraeli achieved success by his own
      efforts, but that he is extremely conceited.
   Intended to cause laughter at and scorn for Disraeli.
   Provides evidence that the speaker scorns Disraeli
      and also that the speaker is witty.

16. Asserts that wisdom is imputed to a silent man.
    Intended to cause people to stop chattering.
    Provides evidence that the speaker esteems silence
        (at least in others!) and is not always silent
        himself.
17. Asserts that well chosen words are very valuable.
    Intended to cause people to speak well.
    Provides evidence that the speaker esteems eloquence
        and is himself eloquent.
18. Asserts that the speaker is hostile to tyranny.
    Intended to cause all others who oppose tyranny to
        give political support to the speaker.
    Provides evidence that the speaker is hostile to
        tyranny, eloquent, and religious.
19. Asserts that a free man does not think of death,
        and that a wise man thinks of life.
    Intended to cause people to stop worrying about death.
    Provides evidence that the speaker is more concerned
        with life than with death.
21. Asserts that egoism is generally the reason why a
        person who is reasonably well off does not enjoy
        life.
    Intended to cause people to take an active interest
        in others.
    Provides evidence that the speaker dislikes egoism and
        takes an interest in others.
22. Asserts that young and inexperienced men cannot profit
        from the study of political science, because its
        end is reasoned action whereas a young man is
        guided by passion rather than reason.
    Intended to cause teachers of political science not
        to accept young and inexperienced men as pupils.
    Provides evidence that the speaker is not a young man.
23. Asserts that free discussion of a question is helpful
        to discovering its correct answer.
    Intended to cause people to discuss issues freely and
        to overthrow any institutions that tend to suppress
        freedom of discussion.
    Provides evidence that the speaker is in favor of
        freedom of discussion.
24. Asserts that struggle (=war) makes men strong, and that
        eternal peace would cause mankind to perish.
    Intended to cause people to support the nation's wars.
    Provides evidence that the speaker is warlike (and
        uninformed?)
25. Asserts that the speaker is not eloquent.
    Intended to cause his hearers to believe what the
        speaker says.
    Provides evidence that the speaker is eloquent.

41

Exercises on pages 78-81
2. Agreement in belief that Mr. Blank's opinions are not
    university shared.
    Disagreement in attitude toward Mr. Blank: a approves
    and b disapproves.
3. Agreement in belief that Ms. Dash contributed five
    dollars.
    Disagreement in attitude toward Ms. Dash's contribution:
    a approves and b disapproves.
4. Agreement in belief that Mr. Dash did not completely
    fill his quota.
    Disagreement in attitude toward Mr. Dash's performance:
    a tends to approve and b disapproves.
6. Disagreement in belief: a believes that Ms. Roe did
    speak at the meeting, and b believes that Ms.
    Roe did not speak at the meeting.
    Agreement in attitude: both have an attitude of dis-
    approval toward Ms. Roe's conduct at the meeting.
7. Disagreement in belief: a believes that Ms. Doe served
    a small meal, and b believes that Ms. Doe served
    a large meal. (See parenthetical remark in solu-
    tion to 5 above in the textbook.)
    Agreement in attitude: both have an attitude of dis-
    approval toward the meal served.
8. Agreement in belief that the contents of the bottle
    are 50% depleted.
    Disagreement in attitude: a seems to like the bottle
    better than b does. (This is one of the old
    chestnuts about the difference between an opti-
    mist and a pessimist.)
9. Agreement in belief that little Jimmy is not bound by
    convention in his efforts to win.
    Disagreement in attitude toward Jimmy's behavior: a
    either approves or is neutral, and b disapproves.
11. Disagreement in belief: a believes that a person has
    only one opportunity to do a particular thing,
    whereas b believes there will always be another
    such opportunity.
    Disagreement in attitude: a is more anxious about
    lost opportunities, b is more relaxed because of
    his confidence that no option is ever permanently
    foreclosed.
12. Agreement in belief that timely action is better than
    delayed action.
    Disagreement in attitude: a seems to be more committed
    to timely action than b is.
13. Disagreement in belief about the strength of affection
    for someone not present: a believes the strength
    increases, b that it diminishes and disappears.

42

Disagreement in attitude is implied here: a is more
likely than b to approve the separation of friends
whose friendship is approved; b is more likely
than a to approve the separation of friends whose
friendship is disapproved.

14. Disagreement in belief: a holds that the better
qualified don't prevail over the less qualified,
whereas b holds that they probably do (or will).

Disagreement in attitude: b approves of effort, pre-
paration, and self-reliance, whereas a does not.

16. Disagreement in belief: Rice believes that enthu-
siasm and good sportsmanship are most valuable
and will ultimately be rewarded, and that winning
is not important. Lombardi does not believe that,
but holds that winning is the only important
thing.

Disagreement in attitude: Rice is concerned with how
you played the game, Lombardi couldn't care less.

17. Disagreement in belief: Aristotle believes that
slavery is necessary and expedient, and also in
accord with innate differences in ability among
humans. Rousseau denies that there are such innate differences among humans as would "justify"
slavery, believing instead that slavishness is
the result of corrupting those enslaved by force.
By implication it is clear that Rousseau would
deny that slavery is either necessary or expedient.

Disagreement in attitude: Aristotle approves of
slavery, admires the master, and despises the
slave. Rousseau abominates slavery, despises the
master, and pities the slave.

18. Disagreement in belief: Mussolini believes that war
stimulates and ennobles those who have the
courage to face it. Sumner believes that war
diminishes justice, happiness, and whatever is
noble ("God-like") in people.

Disagreement in attitude: Mussolini approves of war,
Sumner disapproves of it.

19. Disagreement in belief about the importance and the
consequences of education: Garfield believes
it is next in importance to freedom and justice,
for which it is necessary; Moore believes it is
unimportant--or that its elimination is important, because education destroys artistic
feeling, drives clerks to drink, and makes no
contribution to learning.

Disagreement in attitude: Garfield esteems education,
Moore disapproves of it.

21. Agreement in belief that there is room and need for
improvement in the practice of agriculture.

43

Disagreement in attitude toward the agricultural
life: Washington approves and Russell disapproves.
22. Disagreement in belief: Jefferson believes that under
certain circumstances (the existence of unculti-
vated land and unemployed poor) the laws of private property conflict with natural rights, and
Pope Leo XIII believes that the laws of private
property are in full accord with natural rights,
without exception.
Disagreement in attitude: under certain circumstances
Jefferson disapproves of private property, under
all circumstances Pope Leo XIII approves of it.
23. Disagreement in belief: Grant believes that there is
a right to revolt under certain circumstances,
and by implication, a right to incite to revolt
under those circumstances; whereas Pope Leo XIII
believes that there is no right to incite to
revolt, and by implication, no right to revolt,
under any circumstances.
Disagreement in attitude: Grant approves of revolution under some circumstances, Pope Leo XIII
disapproves of revolution under all circumstances.
24. Disagreement in belief: Coleridge believes that
language embodies past human achievements and is
the means to our future conquests; Hawthorne
believes that   is not true, because human language is no better than animal sounds.
26. Nothing having to do with belief is here in question:
Stobaeus is obviously not speaking literally,
for sustenance comes of the reaping and sowing;
and Jefferson is merely expressing his feeling
for farming.
Disagreement in attitude: Stobaeus disapproves of
farming, or at least expresses a flippant, pe-
jorative attitude toward it; Jefferson approves
heartily.
27. Agreement in belief that our country is our country
right or wrong, and belief that our country may
be wrong on occasion. Possible disagreement
in belief about what ought to be done on the
latter occasions: Decatur says nothing about
them whereas Schurz says that when wrong it ought
to be put right.
Agreement in patriotic attitude with Decatur more
vehement than Schurz. Disagreement in attitude
with Decatur more accepting of what the country
does whereas Schurz feels greater individual
responsibility for the country's actions.
28. Disagreement in belief as to the relative values of
peace and war: Tacitus says that some kinds of

peace are worse than war; Erasmus says any kind
of peace is better than any kind of war.
    Disagreement in attitude: Tacitus approves of some
        kinds of war and disapproves of some kinds of
        peace; Erasmus disapproves of all war and approves
        of every kind of peace.
29. Disagreement in belief about how pleasant farms are:
        Thoreau believes that they are not, Everett be-
        lieves that they are.
    Disagreement in attitude toward farms: Thoreau dis-
        approves, Everett approves.
30. Disagreement in belief: St. Aubyn believes that clear
        thinking (=reason) develops the full potentiali-
        ties of the mind and is the only way to avoid
        disaster. Luther believes that reason is the
        enemy of faith and promotes disaster by opposing
        religion.
    Disagreement in attitude: St. Aubyn approves of
        reason, Luther disapproves.

Exercises on pages 101-109
    2. Ignoratio Elenchi (irrelevant conclusion) 3. Petitio
Principii (begging the question) 4. Argumentum ad Hominen
(both abusive and circumstantial) 6. Argumentum ad
Verecundiam (appeal to authority) It might be argued that
because Freud is a psychologist, questions of "belief"
fall within the area of his special competence. I think
that argument would be dead wrong: unless the words
'educated' and 'belief' are being used in some special
and outrageous sense, the fact that millions of highly
educated people have sincere religious belief proves it
is possible--and that Freud is arguing a theological
rather than a psychological issue here. 7. Ignoratio
Elenchi (irrelevant conclusion)--purporting to argue for
the conclusion that all groups have leaders, Ms. says
that if there are no leaders in a task-oriented group then
the task does not get accomplished. 8. Argumentum ad
Hominem (abusive) 9. False Cause 11. Petitio Principii
(begging the question) 12. Argumentum ad Hominen (circumstantial) committed by "one evening newspaper" which
divided a column of its own into double columns...Argumen-
tum ad Hominem (abusive) committed by Mr. Quintus Slide
in his reply. 13. Argumentum ad Hominem (abusive) 14.
Ignoratio Elenchi (irrelevant conclusion) 16. Petitio
Principii (begging the question) 17. Argumentum ad
Populum 18. Argumentum ad Ignorantiam (argument from
ignorance) 19. Argumentum ad Baculum (appeal to force)
21. Argumentum ad Hominem (circumstantial) 22. Argumentum ad Populum 23. Argumentum ad Ignorantiam (argument from ignorance) 24. Complex Question, perhaps also
False Cause 26. Accident 27. Argumentum ad Baculum

(appeal to force--or deprivation, in this case) 28. Argumentum ad Ignorantiam (argument from ignorance) 29. Argumentum ad Misericordiam (appeal to pity) 31. Argumentum ad Hominem (circumstantial and/or abusive) 32. Complex Question 33. Converse Accident (hasty generalization) and Accident 34. False Cause 36. Argumentum ad Hominem (circumstantial) "Poisoning the Well" 37. Accident 38. False Cause 39. Argumentum ad Baculum (appeal to force) 41. Argumentum ad Misericordiam (appeal to pity) 42. Ignoratio Elenchi (irrelevant conclusion) 43. Converse Accident (hasty generalization) 44. Argumentum ad Hominem (abusive) 46. Argumentum ad Ignorantiam (argument from ignorance) 47. Argumentum ad Hominem (abusive) 48. Argumentum ad Hominem (circumstantial) 49. Argumentum ad Baculum (appeal to force--or eviction, in this case) 50. False Cause

Exercises on pages 117-119

2. Equivocation (on "poor") 3. Equivocation (on "Nobody") 4. Composition 6. Amphiboly 7. Composition 8. Equivocation (on "third child") or (possibly) Division. 9. Equivocation (on "distinguished") 11. Equivocation (on "no news") 12. Division 13. Composition 14. Equivocation 16. Division 17. Accent (quoting out of context) 18. Division 19. Equivocation (on "rare") 20. Division 21. Amphiboly

Exercises on pages 120-125

2. Argumentum ad Hominem (abusive) 3. Division 4. Petitio Principii 6. Accent (no more money) 7. Argumentum ad Hominem (abusive) 8. Accident 9. Argumentum ad Ignorantiam 11. Argumentum ad Hominem (abusive) 12. Equivocation (on "departure from law") 13. Converse Accident 14. Composition 16. Division 17. False Cause 18. Complex Question 19. Accident 21. Argumentum ad Hominem (circumstantial) 22. Equivocation (on "taste" and "tasty") 23. Petitio Principii or the passage might be interpreted not as an argument at all, but as giving directions on where to look for something, together with an explanation of why one should look there. 24. Petitio Principii 26. Equivocation (on "found") 27. Complex Question 28. Composition 29. Argumentum ad Baculum or (possibly) Argumentum ad Hominem (circumstantial) 31. Converse Accident 32. Argumentum ad Hominem (abusive or (possibly) circumstantial) 33. Accident 34. Amphiboly 36. Accident or (possibly) Composition 37. Complex Question 38. Argumentum ad Verecundiam 39. Argumentum ad Misericordiam 41. Accident 42. Argumentum ad Hominem (abusive) 43. Division 44. Equivocation (on "right") 46. Ignoratio Elenchi (irrelevant conclusion) 47. Argumentum ad Hominem (abusive) 48. Equivocation (on "knows most") or (possibly) not a fallacy but simply an argument

with false premises   49.   Equivocation (on "nothing")
or Amphiboly   50.   Division   51.   Division   52.   Ignoratio
Elenchi (irrelevant conclusion), or perhaps False Cause,
or possibly Accident

Exercises on pages 132-135

2.   An apparently verbal dispute that is really genuine.
     The ambiguous word "relevant" is used by Daye in
     the sense of <u>dealing with eternally recurring</u>
     <u>problems and values such as love and sacrifice,</u>
     <u>the conflict of generations, life and death,</u>
     and by Knight in the sense of <u>dealing with the</u>
     <u>pressing and immediate issues of our time:</u>
     <u>inflation, unemployment, the population explosion,</u>
     <u>and the energy crisis.</u> Behind the verbal dispute
     there is very probably a disagreement in attitude,
     with Daye esteeming the plays of Sophocles more
     highly than Knight does.

3.   An obviously genuine dispute.   Daye and Knight have
     quite different criteria for excellence in fathers,
     but there is no evidence that any words are used
     by them in different senses.   They obviously
     disagree in attitude.

4.   An obviously genuine dispute about whether earnings
     are up or down.   Daye and Knight evidently have
     different data upon which their statements are
     based.   There may be a disagreement in attitude
     toward the company, but that is not clear.

6.   An apparently verbal dispute that is really genuine.
     The ambiguous phrase "excellent student" is used
     by Daye in the sense of <u>student with a high level</u>
     <u>of interest and class participation</u> and by Knight
     in the sense of <u>student who is punctual in turning</u>
     <u>in assignments.</u> They disagree in attitude toward
     Ann, Daye approving and Knight disapproving.

7.   Merely verbal.   The ambiguous phrase "done of one's own
     free will" is used by Daye to characterize an
     action not constrained by external pressure and
     accompanied by deliberation, but by Knight to
     characterize only actions that are completely
     uncaused.

8.   An apparently verbal dispute that is really genuine.
     The ambiguous phrase "productive scholar" is used
     by Daye in the sense of one who publishes ex-
     tensively, and by Knight in the sense of one who
     produces new ideas or discoveries.   They really
     disagree in attitude, Daye approving and Knight
     disapproving Professor Graybeard.

9.   Merely verbal.   The ambiguous word "new" is used by
     Daye in the sense of <u>different</u> and by Knight in
     the sense of <u>not previously used</u>.   There does

not seem to be any particular disagreement in attitude.

11. Merely verbal. The ambiguous phrase "long way" is used by Daye in the sense of "taking nearly two hours to walk" and ,by Knight in the sense of "taking (much?) more than ten minutes to drive."

12. Apparently verbal dispute that is really genuine, ambiguous phrase "liberal" used by Daye in the sense of <u>favoring progress or reform</u> and by Knight in the sense of giving <u>freely or in ample measure</u>. They really disagree in attitude toward Gray, Daye approving and Knight disapproving of him.

13. Obviously genuine: can be regarded either as a disagreement in belief, with Daye affirming and Knight denying the proposition that <u>the amount of emphasis given to athletics at The University of Winnemac</u> is excessive, or as a disagreement in attitude, Daye disapproving and Knight approving the amount of emphasis placed on athletics at The University of Winnemac.

14. Apparently verbal dispute that is really genuine, ambiguous phrase "bad taste" used by Daye in the sense of <u>indecorous</u>, <u>improper</u>, or <u>unseemly</u>, and by Knight in the sense of <u>being without flavor or unpleasant to eat</u>. They really disagree in attitude toward the menu in question, Daye disapproving and Knight approving.

16. Obviously genuine, with Daye affirming and Knight denying the proposition that the <u>average intelligence of college graduates is higher than that of college freshmen</u>. (Both their arguments, however, leave much to be desired).

17. Merely verbal, ambiguous word "sound" used by Daye in the sense of <u>auditory sensation</u> and by Knight in the sense of <u>longitudinal vibrational energy</u>.

18. Merely verbal, ambiguous phrase "more plentiful" (as applied to money) used by Daye in the (quite common) sense of <u>greater amounts of money available for borrowing</u>, and by Knight in the (quite uncommon) sense of <u>greater amounts of money that physically exist</u>.

19. Apparently verbal dispute that is really genuine, ambiguous word "Christian" used by Daye in the sense of <u>one who exemplifies in his life the moral teachings of Jesus</u> and by Knight in the sense of <u>one who belongs to and regularly attends a Christian church</u>. They really disagree in attitude toward Mr. G., Daye approving and Knight disapproving of him.

48

EXERCISES ON PAGES 135-153

20. A tricky example for which alternative analyses are plausible. One plausible treatment is to regard it as an obviously genuine dispute, with Daye denying and Knight affirming the proposition that <u>Knight should ask his wife</u>. Another plausible treatment is to regard it as an apparently verbal dispute that is really genuine, with the ambiguous phrase "your own judgment" (about it) used by Daye in the sense of <u>deciding about it without considering anyone else's opinion</u> and by Knight in the (broader) sense of <u>deciding everything about it including the question of whether or not to consult the opinions of others</u> - with Daye and Knight really disagreeing in belief as explained in the first "treatment."

Exercises on page 147

I. 2. beverage, alcoholic beverage, wine, white wine, fine white wine, champagne.
    3. athlete, ballplayer, baseball player, fielder, infielder, shortstop.
    4. dairy product, milk derivative, cheese, soft cheese, strong soft cheese, limburger.
    5. number, real number, rational number, integer, positive integer, prime.
II. 1. aquatic animal, fish, game fish, pike, muskellunge.
    2. domestic animal, beast of burden, horse, foal, filly.
    3. liquid, beverage, liquor, brandy, cognac.
    4. instrument, musical instrument, string instrument, violin, Stradivarius.
    5. polygon, quadrilateral, parrallelogram, rectangle, square.

Exercises on page 150

I. 2. Joe Frazier, Jimmy Ellis, Muhammed Ali
    3. Bach, Beethoven, Brahms
    4. Shakespeare, Marlowe, Ben Jonson
    6. Tulip, Gladioli, Dahlia
    7. Washington, Grant, Eisenhower
    8. New York, San Francisco, Duluth
    9. Eli Whitney, Thomas Edison, Robert Fulton
    10. Browning, Keats, Shelley
II. 2. Heavyweight champions
    3. Germans
    4. Elizabethans
    6. Bulbs
    7. United States Presidents
    8. American cities
    9. Americans
    10. Victorians

Exercises on pages 153-154

I. 2. clown 3. graveyard 4. autocrat 6. banquet

7. attic 8. hurry 9. baby 11. cows 12. maze
13. beggar 14. tyro 16. cure-all 17. charlatan
18. platform 19. villain 20. wigwam

II. 2. very large meal 3. young man 4. male sibling 6. young horse 7. female offspring 8. female sheep 9. male parent 11. young woman 12. married man 13. young sheep 14. female horse 16. female parent 17. very small horse 18. male sheep 19. female sibling 21. male offspring 22. unmarried woman 23. male horse 24. married woman

Exercises on pages 158-162

I. adequately supplied by any good dictionary.
II.
2. too broad, because a casual opinion may just <u>happen</u> to be true; Rule 3.
3. figurative language; Rule 4.
4. circular; Rule 2.
6. negative where it could be affirmative; Rule 5. Also too broad, since inanimate objects lack all intents; Rule 3.
7. figurative language; Rule 4.
8. circular; Rule 2.
9. too narrow, because not all paintings are pictures, not all paintings are on canvas, not all are drawn with a brush; Rule 3.
11. too broad, because there are such <u>individual</u> (private) acts of violence which would not be called "wars"; Rule 3.
12. too narrow, because there are rubber and treated cloth raincoats; Rule 3.
13. circular, Rule 2.
14. too broad, because a snort is not a sneeze, and too narrow, because some sneezes are inaudible; Rule 3.
16. too narrow, because there are works of art which transmit feelings other than the highest and best, and abstract works which would seem not intended to transmit <u>any</u> feelings, and private or secret works which are not intended to transmit to others at all; Rule 3. It probably does not state the essence; if we can believe theories of art that regard the essence as pleasure (objectified), beauty, unity-in-complexity, etc.; Rule 1.
17. not really a definition by genus and difference: is "when" a genus?
18. too narrow, because some clouds are opaque, and some have textures that are not fleecy; Rule 3.
19. circular, Rule 2.
20. obscure language: how can that which "dependeth not on the imagination" fill "imagined place"? Rule 4.

III. 2. figurative language; Rule 4. Also too narrow, because
          one may have faith without knowing the truth or
          falsehood of that in which faith is put, or be-
          cause if one knows something not to be true one
          cannot believe it; Rule 3.
      3. figurative language; Rule 4. Also too narrow, be-
          cause one may have faith in something probable;
          Rule 3.
      4. too narrow, because some poetry is not "widely effec-
          tive" on account of its obscurity; Rule 3.
      6. figurative language; Rule 4.
      7. figurative language; Rule 4.
      8. figurative language; Rule 4.
      9. too broad, because it may occasionally be very expe-
          dient to think or believe a falsehood, and too
          narrow, because it may sometimes be inexpedient
          to think or believe a truth; Rule 3. It may
          also be criticized for not stating the essence
          and thus violating Rule 1, but here we have a
          philosophical controversy.
     11. possibly circular; Rule 2. But possibly not, if the
          term "economic activities" has already been
          adequately defined.
     12. too broad? too narrow? Rule 2? Fails to state
          the essence? Rule 1?
     13. too narrow in the case where the subjects are sover-
          eign, as in a democracy; Rule 3.
     14. too narrow, because there are "useless" goods, and
          perhaps too broad in case there are useful
          evils; Rule 3.
     16. figurative language; Rule 4. Also too narrow, because
          not all beliefs are really part of our "in-
          tellectual life;" Rule 3.
     17. too narrow, because there may still be political
          power in a classless society--to keep the peace,
          deal with other communities, etc. Rule 3.
     18. too narrow, because some calamities are not "like"
          anything that could befall the pitier; Rule 3.
     19. circular, Rule 2. Also too narrow, because justice
          is not a mere "kind of state of character;"
          Rule 3.
     21. figurative language, Rule 4.
     22. figurative language, Rule 4.
     23. obscure language; Rule 4.
     24. perhaps too narrow in its claim that the aim of tragedy
          is catharsis of pity and fear, which would violate
          Rule 3. But almost as many scholars would de-
          fend Aristotle's definition as would criticize it.
     25. figurative language, Rule 4. Probably the definition
          of "liberty" is too narrow in several respects:

it is not confined to people in "good social
position", or to saying what "everybody believes;" Rule 3. And "license" is also defined
in a way that is too narrow, because often people
exercise license by saying what is not true;
Rule 3. But this kind of comment runs the danger
of spoiling a good joke.

26. although this is a very illuminating "definition", it
is probably too narrow, because some insights of
female intuition can not only be examined syllo-
gistically but can pass such examination; Rule 3.

27. this is a beautiful definition; if a fault is to be
found it is that people can be patriotic to only
some civic groups such as a nation, which if
true would make Sumner's definition too broad;
Rule 3.

Exercises on page 169

2. E: S = athletes who have ever accepted pay for
participating in sports; P = amateurs.

3. E: S = dogs which are without pedigrees; P = candidates for blue ribbons in official dog shows
which are sponsored by the American Kennel Society.

4. A: S = satellites which are presently in orbits
less than ten thousand miles high; P = very delicate devices that cost many thousands of dollars to
manufacture.

6. O: S = paintings produced by artists who are uni-
versally recognized as masters; P = works of genuine
merit that either are or deserve to be preserved in
museums and made available to the public.

7. A: S = drivers of automobiles which are not safe;
P = desperadoes who threaten the lives of their
fellow men.

8. I: S = politicians who could not be elected to the
most minor positions; P = appointed officials in
our government today.

9. O: S = drugs which are very effective when they
are properly administered; P = safe remedies that
all medicine cabinets should contain.

10. E: S = men who have not themselves done creative
work in the arts; P = responsible critics on whose
judgment we can rely.

Exercises on page 173

2. Affirmative, universal. Subject term distributed,
predicate term undistributed.

3. Negative, particular. Subject term undistributed,
predicate term distributed.

4. Affirmative, particular. Subject and predicate
terms both undistributed.

6. Affirmative, universal. Subject term distributed,

52

predicate term undistributed.
7. Affirmative, particular. Subject and predicate terms both undistributed.
8. Negative, universal. Subject and predicate terms both distributed.
9. Negative, particular. Subject term undistributed, predicate term distributed.
10. Affirmative, universal. Subject term distributed, predicate term undistributed.

Exercises on pages 177-178
2. If (a) is true: (b) is false, (c) is true, (d) is false; if (a) is false: (b) is true, (c) and (d) are undetermined.
3. If (a) is true: (b) and (c) are undetermined, (d) is false; if (a) is false: (b) is true, (c) is false, (d) is true.
4. If (a) is true: (b) is false, (c) and (d) are undetermined; if (a) is false: (b) is true, (c) is false, (d) is true.

Exercises on pages 183-187
I. 2. All commissioned officers in the United States Army are graduates of West Point. Not in general equivalent.
3. Some overpriced and under-powered automobiles are European cars. Equivalent.
4. No warm blooded animals are reptiles. Equivalent.
5. Some elderly persons who would be incapable of doing an honest day's work are professional wrestlers. Equivalent.
II. 2. All organic compounds are non-metals.
3. Some clergymen are non-abstainers.
4. All geniuses are nonconformists.
5. No objects suitable for boat anchors are objects weighing less than fifteen pounds.
III. 2. Some nonofficers are not nonsoldiers. Equivalent.
3. All degenerates are nonscholars. Equivalent.
4. All objects more than four feet high are things weighing at least fifty pounds. Equivalent.
5. Some residents are not citizens. Equivalent.
IV. 2. true 3. undetermined 4. true 6. true 7. undetermined 8. false 9. undetermined 10. false.
V. 2. true 3. false 4. false 6. false 7. true 8. false 9. true 10. false
VI. 2. undetermined 3. undetermined 4. undetermined
6. undetermined 7. undetermined 8. undetermined
9. false 11. undetermined 12. undetermined
13. undetermined 14. undetermined 16. undetermined
17. undetermined 18. undetermined 19. undetermined

53

	21.	undetermined	22.	undetermined	23.	true
	24.	undetermined	26.	false	27.	undetermined
	28.	undetermined	29.	undetermined	30.	undetermined
	31.	undetermined				
VII.	2.	undetermined	3.	undetermined	4.	undetermined
	6.	undetermined	7.	undetermined	8.	undetermined
	9.	undetermined	11.	undetermined	12.	undetermined
	13.	undetermined	14.	undetermined	16.	undetermined
	17.	undetermined	18.	undetermined	19.	true
	21.	undetermined	22.	undetermined	23.	undetermined
	24.	undetermined	26.	false	27.	undetermined
	28.	false	29.	undetermined	30.	undetermined
	31.	undetermined				

Exercises on pages 190-191

II. step (3) to (4) is invalid (subalternation)
III. step (2) to (3) is invalid (subalternation)
IV. step (1) to (2) is invalid (assumes A and E to be contraries)
V. Step (1) to (2) is invalid (assumes I and O to be subcontraries)

Exercises on page 197

2. PM = 0   P   M
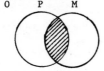

3. M$\bar{S}$ = 0   M   S

4. M$\bar{P}$ ≠ 0   M   P
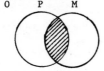

6. PS ≠ 0   P   S
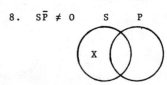

7. P$\bar{M}$ = 0   P   M
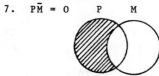

8. S$\bar{P}$ ≠ 0   S   P

9. P$\bar{S}$ = 0   P   S
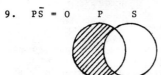

11. SM ≠ 0   S   M
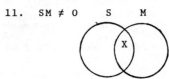

54

12. $M\bar{P} = 0$ M   P

13. $S\bar{P} \neq 0$ S   P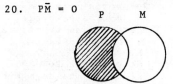

14. $MP = 0$ M   P

16. $P\bar{S} \neq 0$ P   S

17. $PM \neq 0$ P   M

18. $S\bar{M} \neq 0$ S   M

19. $PS = 0$ P   S

20. $P\bar{M} = 0$ P   M

Exercises on pages 201-202

2. Some objects of worship are fir trees.
   All fir trees are evergreens.
   Therefore some evergreens are objects of worship.
   IAI-4

3. Some artificial satellites are not American inventions.
   All artificial satellites are important scientific
       achievements.
   Therefore some important scientific achievements are not
       American inventions.
   OAO-3

4. All certified public accountants are people of good
       business sense.
   No television stars are certified public accountants.
   Therefore no television stars are people of good
       business sense.
   AEE-1

6. No expensive and delicate mechanisms are suitable toys
       for children.

All hi-fi sets are expensive and delicate mechanisms.
Therefore no hi-fi sets are suitable toys for children.
    EAE-1
7 Some juvenile delinquents are products of broken homes.
   All juvenile delinquents are maladjusted individuals.
   Therefore some maladjusted individuals are products
       of broken homes.
    IAI-3
8. Some well informed people are stubborn individuals
       who never admit a mistake.
   No stubborn individuals who never admit a mistake
       are good teachers.
   Therefore some good teachers are not well informed
       people.
    IEO-4
9. All proteins are organic compounds.
   All enzymes are organic compounds.
   Therefore all enzymes are proteins.
    AAA-2
10. All automobiles designed for family use are vehicles
        intended to be driven at moderate speeds.
    No sports cars are vehicles intended to be driven at
        moderate speeds.
    Therefore no sports cars are automobiles designed for
        family use.
    AEE-2

Exercises on pages 204-205

2. Valid 3. No dogs are reptiles, so some reptiles are
mammals, since some mammals are not dogs. 4. No dogs are
cats, but all cats are mammals, so no dogs are mammals.
6. Valid 7. Some mammals are not house pets, so some dogs
are not mammals, since some dogs are not house pets. 8. No
animals are cats, because no dogs are cats and some animals
are dogs. 9. Valid. 10. All square circles are circles,
and all square circles are squares, therefore some circles
are squares.

Exercises on pages 214-215

I. 2. No P is M.   S   P   valid.
        Some S is M.
        ∴ Some S is not P.

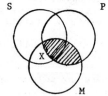

3. Some M is not P.
    All M is S.
    ∴ Some S is not P.

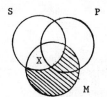

valid.

4. All P is M.
    Some M is not S.
    ∴ Some S is not P.

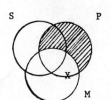

invalid.

6. Some P is not M.
    All S is M.
    ∴ Some S is not P.

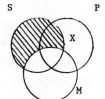

invalid.

7. All M is P.
    Some S is not M.
    ∴ Some S is not P.

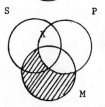

invalid.

8. No M is P.
    All M is S.
    ∴ No S is P.

invalid.

9. No M is P.
    Some M is S.
    ∴ Some S is not P.

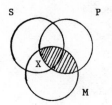

valid.

11. All M is P.
    Some M is not S.
    ∴ Some S is not P.

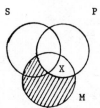

invalid.

12. No M is P.
    All S is M.
    ∴ No S is P.

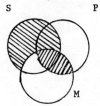

valid.

13. Some M is P.
    All S is M.
    ∴ Some S is P.

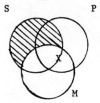

invalid.

14. Some P is not M.
    All M is S.
    ∴ Some S is not P.

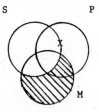

invalid.

15. No M is P.
Some S is M.
∴ Some S is not P.

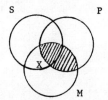

valid.

II. 2. Some philosophers are mathematicians.
All scientists are mathematicians.
∴ Some scientists are
philosophers.

IAI-2
invalid.

3. No gases are argon compounds.
All argon compounds are metals.
∴ Some metals are not
gases.

EAO-4
invalid

4. All criminals are parasites.
Some neurotics are not
parasites.
∴ Some neurotics are
not criminals.

A0O-2
valid

59

EXERCISES ON PAGE 215

6. No pioneers were unsavory
    persons.
    All criminals are un-
    savory persons.
    ∴ No criminals were
    pioneers.

C   P   valid

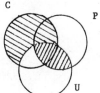

EAE-2

7. All musicians are baseball
    fans.
    No musicians are astro-
    nauts.
    ∴ No astronauts are
    baseball fans.

A   B   invalid

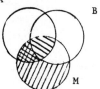

AEE-3

8. Some Protestants are not
    Methodists.
    Some Christians are not
    Protestants.
    ∴ Some Christians are
    not Methodists.

C   M   000-1
                                             invalid

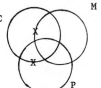

9. All active politicians
    are people whose
    primary interest is
    in winning elections.
    No people whose primary
    interest is in win-
    ning elections are
    true liberals.
    ∴ No true liberals are
    active politicians.

T   A   AEE-4
                                             valid

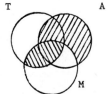

60

10. All labor leaders are
true liberals.
No weaklings are true
liberals.
∴ No weaklings are
labor leaders.

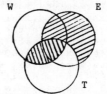

W   E   AEE-2

valid

T

Exercises on pages 221-223
   I.   2.   Affirmative Conclusion from a Negative Premiss,
            breaks Rule 5.
      3.   Illicit Major, breaks Rule 3.
      4.   Exclusive Premisses, breaks Rule 4.
      6.   Undistributed Middle, breaks Rule 2.
      7.   Illicit Minor, breaks Rule 3; and Affirmative
            Conclusion from a Negative Premiss, breaks Rule 5.
      8.   Existential Fallacy, breaks Rule 6.
      9.   Affirmative Conclusion from a Negative Premiss,
            breaks Rule 5.
    11.   Existential Fallacy, breaks Rule 6.
    12.   Undistributed Middle, breaks Rule 2.
    13.   Exclusive Premisses, breaks Rule 4.
    14.   Illicit Major, breaks Rule 3.
    15.   Illicit Minor, breaks Rule 3.
  II.   2.   Four Terms (equivocation on "criminal actions"),
            breaks Rule 1.
      3.   Exclusive Premisses, breaks Rule 4.
      4.   Illicit Minor, breaks Rule 3.
      6.   Affirmative Conclusion from a Negative Premiss,
            breaks Rule 5.
      7.   Illicit Major, breaks Rule 3.
      8.   Undistributed Middle, breaks Rule 2.
      9.   Four Terms (equivocation on "most hungry," which is
            used to mean most hungry before eating in the
            major premiss, and to mean most hungry after
            eating in the minor premiss), breaks Rule 1.
    10.   Illicit Minor, breaks Rule 3.
 III.   2.   Undistributed Middle, breaks Rule 2.
      3.   Illicit Major, breaks Rule 3.
      4.   Existential Fallacy, breaks Rule 6.
      6.   Exclusive Premisses, breaks Rule 4; and Affirmative
            Conclusion from a Negative Premiss, breaks Rule
            5.
      7.   Four Terms ("democrats" and "Democrats" are two
            different terms), breaks Rule 1.
      8.   Illicit Minor, breaks Rule 3.
      9.   Illicit Major, breaks Rule 3.

10. Four Terms (equivocation on "people who like it," which has a different meaning in the conclusion than it has in the premiss), breaks Rule 1.

IV. 2. AA- and AE- violate Rule 6; AIO violates Rule 3; AOI violates Rule 5; AOO violates Rule 3. EA- and EE- violate Rule 6; EII violates Rule 5; EO- violates Rule 4. IA- and II- violate Rule 2; IEI violates Rule 5; IEO violates Rule 3; IOI violates Rule 5; IOO violates Rule 3. OA- and OI- violate Rule 2; OE- and OO- violate Rule 4. Therefore only moods AII and EIO are valid here.

3. In Figure 3 both premisses would have to be negative in violation of Rule 4. In all other figures (1, 2, 4) it is possible as is shown by the validity of EAE-1, EAE-2, and AEE-4.

4. None. Regardless of figure, II- would violate Rule 2 and OO- would violate Rule 4. If one premiss is I and one is O then by Rule 5 the conclusion would be negative and would distribute its predicate. By Rule 3 the major term would have to be distributed in the major premiss, but since I and O distribute only one term, Rule 2 would then be violated.

6. None. By Rule 2 one of the distributed terms would have to be the middle term. One premiss would have to distribute both its terms and would have to be an E. Then by Rule 5 the conclusion would have to be negative and since it is to distribute only one of its terms it would have to be an O. The other premiss is to distribute only the middle term and so could be only an A or an O. But it could not be an A by Rule 6 and it could not be an O by Rule 4.

7. None. The negative conclusion could not be an E, for if it were then by Rule 3 both major and minor terms would have to be distributed in the premisses, and since an affirmative proposition distributes at most one of its terms, Rule 2 would be violated. Nor could the negative conclusion be an O, for if it were then by Rule 6 at least one premiss would have to be particular, and therefore an I. But an I proposition distributes neither of its terms, so both premisses would distribute only one term between them, thus violating either Rule 2 or Rule 3.

8. None. If the particular premiss were an O then by Rule 5 the conclusion would be negative and hence an E, whence by Rule 3 both major and minor terms would have to be distributed in the premisses. Since the middle term must be distributed there also, by Rule 2, and the O premiss distributes only <u>one</u> of its terms, the <u>other</u> premiss would have to distribute both its terms and be an E, thus violating Rule 4.

On the other hand, if the particular premiss were
an I, it would distribute neither of its terms. But
since the universal conclusion requires by Rule 3 that
the minor term be distributed in the minor premiss,
the I premiss would have to be the major premiss,
and, being an I, would not distribute the middle
term. So by Rule 2 the middle term must also be
distributed by the minor premiss, which would therefore have to be an E. Then by Rule 5 the conclusion
would be negative and distribute the major term also,
in violation of Rule 3.

9. By Rule 2 the middle term is distributed in at least
one premiss, hence at least one premiss is negative,
so by Rule 5 the conclusion is negative also and is
an E. Hence by Rule 3 both premisses are universal,
and by Rule 4 at least one is affirmative. Hence the
only two moods are AEE and EAE, both valid in Figure
2.

10. None. In Figure 1 the minor premiss would have to
be negative, whence by Rule 5 the conclusion would be
negative, so by Rule 3 the major premiss would have
to be negative in violation of Rule 4. In Figure 2
both premisses would have to be negative in violation
of Rule 4. In Figure 3 both premisses would have to
be universal, hence by Rule 6 the conclusion would be
universal, so the minor premiss would have to be
negative by Rule 3, and by Rule 5 the conclusion would
be negative, so by Rule 3 the major premiss would have
to be negative also in violation of Rule 4. In
Figure 4 the major premiss would have to be negative,
whence by Rule 5 the conclusion would be negative and
so by Rule 3 the major premiss would be universal,
and since the minor premiss would have to be universal, by Rule 6 the conclusion would be universal,
whence by Rule 3 the minor premiss would have to be
negative also in violation of Rule 4.

11. If the conclusion is A, then neither premiss can be
negative by Rule 5, the minor premiss cannot be I by
Rule 3, and the two premisses cannot be IA without
violating either Rule 2 or Rule 3. Hence the only
possible mood here is AAA, which is valid only in the
first figure, because AAA-2 violates Rule 2 and both
AAA-3 and AAA-4 violate Rule 3. So the only valid
form with A conclusion is AAA-1.
If the conclusion is E, all three terms must be
distributed in the premisses, whence at least one
premiss must be E also. They cannot both be E by
Rule 4, and by the same Rule the other premiss cannot
be O. It cannot be I or Rule 3 would be violated.

Hence the only possible moods here are AEE and EAE.
Rule 3 eliminates AEE-1 and AEE-3, but AEE-2 and
AEE-4 are valid. Rule 3 also eliminates EAE-3 and
EAE-4, but EAE-1 and EAE-2 are valid. So the only
valid forms with an E.conclusion are AEE-2, AEE-4,
EAE-1, and EAE-2.
If the conclusion is I, then neither premiss can be
negative by Rule 5, the premisses cannot be AA by
Rule 6, or II by Rule 2. Hence the only possible
moods here are AII and IAI. Rule 2 eliminates AII-2
and AII-4, but AII-1 and AII-3 are valid. Rule 2
also eliminates IAI-1 and IAI-2, but IAI-3 and IAI-4
are valid. So the only valid forms with an I conclusion are AII-1, AII-3, IAI-3, and IAI-4.
If the conclusion is O, then by Rule 3 the major premiss cannot be I. If the major premiss is A then
the minor premiss cannot be either A or E without
violating Rule 6, and it cannot be an I without
violating either Rule 2 or Rule 3. Rule 2 eliminates
AOO-4, and Rule 3 eliminates both AOO-1 and AOO-3.
But AOO-2 is valid. If the major premiss is E, then
the minor premiss cannot be E or O by Rule 4, or A
by Rule 6. But EIO is valid in all four figures. If
the major premiss is O, then the minor premiss cannot
be E or O without violating Rule 4, and it cannot
be I without violating either Rule 2 or Rule 3. Rule
2 eliminates OAO-1, and Rule 3 eliminates OAO-2 and
OAO-4. But OAO-3 is valid. So the only valid forms
with an O conclusion are AOO-2, EIO-1, EIO-2, EIO-3
EIO-4, and OAO-3.
The rules thus eliminate all but the fifteen forms of
standard-form categorical syllogisms indicated.

12. No. If the major term is undistributed in the conclusion, the conclusion must be affirmative, and by
Rule 5, both premisses must be affirmative. If the
major term is distributed in the major premiss, that
premiss - being affirmative - must be the A proposition All P is M and cannot also distribute the middle
term. So the middle term must, by Rule 2, be distributed in the minor premiss, which - being affirmative - must be the A proposition All M is S and cannot
also distribute the minor term. The conclusion cannot
be Some S is P which would violate Rule 6, and it cannot be All S is P which would violate Rule 3. Hence
the major term cannot be distributed in a premiss but
undistributed in the conclusion of a valid syllogism.
If the minor term is undistributed in the conclusion,
the conclusion must be particular.
If it is also affirmative (Some S is P) then by Rule 5
both premisses must be affirmative also. If the minor
64

term is distributed in the minor premiss, that premiss - being affirmative - must be the A proposition
<u>All S is M</u> and cannot also distribute the middle term.
So the middle term must, by Rule 2, be distributed in
the major premiss, which - being affirmative - must
be the A proposition <u>All M is P</u>. But this syllogism
would violate Rule 6.
But if the conclusion is negative (<u>Some S is not P</u>)
it distributes the major term which by Rule 3 must be
distributed in the major premiss. If the minor term
is distributed in the minor premiss, then since by
Rule 2 the middle term must be distributed in at least
one premiss, whichever premiss distributes it must
distribute both its terms and be an E proposition.
The other premiss cannot be negative by Rule 4, and
it cannot be universal by Rule 6, so it must be particular affirmative and hence cannot distribute either
of its terms. This, of course, contradicts the fact
that in this case the major premiss must distribute
the major term and the minor premiss must distribute
the minor term. Hence the minor term cannot be distributed in a premiss but undistributed in the conclusion of a valid syllogism.

Exercises on pages 227-228

2. Some M is R.
    All W is M.
    ∴ Some W is R.

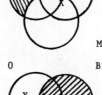

invalid
(Undistribu-
ted Middle)

3. All B is A.
    Some O is not A.
    ∴ Some O is not B.

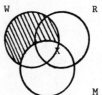

valid

4. No D is P.
    Some P is A.
    ∴ Some A is not D.

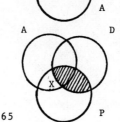

valid

6. All M is C.
    All W is M.
    ∴All W is C.

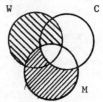

valid

7. All I is C.
    All I is M.
    ∴All M is C.

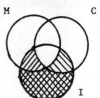

invalid
(Illicit
Minor)

8. All H is M.
    No M is P.
    ∴No P is H.

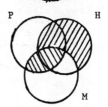

valid

9. No V is P.
    No P is I.
    ∴All I is V.

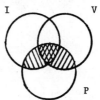

invalid
(Exclusive
Premisses)

10. All O are D.
    No D are U.
    ∴No U are O

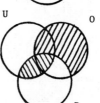

valid

Exercises on page 234
2. No orchids are fragrant things.
3. Some persons are beings who have lived to regret their misspent youths.
4. Some persons worth meeting are not persons worth having as friends.
6. All Ropos are real Havanas.
7. No safe things are exciting things.
8. All winners of the Congressional Medal of Honor are brave people.
9. Some persons are nonappreciators of good counselors. (Or perhaps) Some good counselors are not persons who are appreciated.
11. All persons who hear her sing are inspired persons.
12. All persons who take the sword are persons who shall perish by the sword.
13. All persons who can use the front door are members.
14. All doors that pledges can use are side doors.
16. All candidates of the Old Guard are persons supported by the party regulars. (Or) All party regulars are supporters of any candidate of the Old Guard.
17. All persons who only stand and wait are persons who also serve.
18. All women who know their own limitations are women who are happy indeed.
19. All things of beauty are things that are joys forever.
21. Some glittering things are not gold things.
22. All persons who think the great unhappy are great persons.
23. All persons who never felt wounds are persons who jest at scars. (Always a source of warm discussion!)
24. All things that a man sows are things that that man also reaps.
25. All soft answers are things that turn away wrath.

Exercises on pages 237-241
I. 2. No times when she goes to work are times when she drives her car.
3. All places where he chooses to walk are places where he walks.
4. All times when he orders an item on the menu are times when he orders the most expensive item on the menu. (Or perhaps better) All items on the menu that he orders are items that are the most expensive items on the menu.
6. All places where she may happen to be are places where she tries to sell life insurance.
7. All times when he gets angry are times when he gets red.
8. All occasions on which he is asked to say a few words are occasions on which he talks for hours.
9. All places where reason is left free to combat error of opinion are places where error of opinion may be tolerated.

10. No times when people do not discuss questions freely
    are times when people are most likely to settle
    questions rightly.

II. 2. All predicables are things that come in contradictory
    pairs.
    No names are things that come in contradictory pairs.
    ∴No names are predicables.

AEE-2   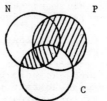   valid

3. All fanaticism is vice.
   All extremism is fanaticism.
   ∴All extremism is vice.

AAA-1   valid

4. All bodies on which a freely swinging pendulum of
   fixed length has periods of oscillation which
   decrease slightly with increasing latitude from
   the equator to both poles   are oblate spheroids
   slightly flattened at the poles.
   The earth is a body on which a freely swinging pendulum
   of fixed length has periods of oscillation which
   decrease slightly with increasing latitude from
   the equator to both poles.
   ∴The earth is an oblate spheroid slightly flattened
   at the poles.

AAA-1   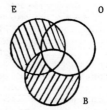   valid

68

6. All times following rain are times fish do not bite.
    This time is a time fish do not bite.
    ∴ This time is a time following rain.

    AAA-2

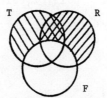

    invalid
    (Undistri-
    buted Middle)

7. All teachers whose values conflict with social norms,
      particularly those of the local community or with
      those of administrators or students or other
      teachers, are persons whose professional lives
      are marked with a pervasive tension.
    All teachers in a pluralistic society dedicated, in
      principle at least, to respect for differences
      among people and to universal education for all,
      are teachers whose values conflict with social
      norms, particularly those of the local community
      or with those of administrators or students or
      other teachers.
    ∴ All teachers in a pluralistic society dedicated, in
      principle at least, to respect for differences
      among people and to universal education for all,
      are persons whose professional lives are marked
      with a pervasive tension.

    AAA-1

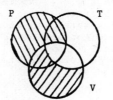

    valid

8. No title contests are dull games.
    The game tomorrow is a title contest.
    ∴ The game tomorrow will not be a dull game.

    EAE-1

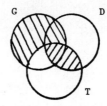

    valid

9. All pairs of persons who contradict each other are pairs
    of persons who cannot both be lying.
    The pair of persons consisting of the first and third
    natives is a pair of persons who contradict each
    other.
    ∴ The pair of persons consisting of the first and third
    natives is a pair of persons who cannot both be
    lying.

    AAA-1   valid

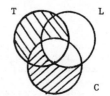

11. All alcoholics are inebriated persons.
    No inebriated persons are dependable persons.
    ∴No dependable persons are alcoholics.

    AEE-4   valid

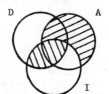

12. All rhapsodes are men who interpret the mind of the poet
    to their hearers.
    No men who interpret the mind of the poet to their
    hearers are men who do not understand the meaning
    of the poet.
    ∴No men who do not understand the meaning of the poet
    are rhapsodes.

    AEE-4   valid

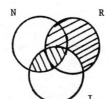

13. No sorrow is a thing that is in God.
    All mercy is sorrow.
    ∴No mercy is a thing that is in God.

      EAE-1 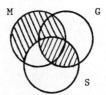 valid

14. No painful sensation is a thing that can exist in an
    unperceiving corporeal substance.
    All intense heat is painful sensation.
    ∴No intense heat is a thing that can exist in an
    unperceiving corporeal substance.

      EAE-1 valid

16. All people are thinkers.
    All bridge players are people.
    ∴All bridge players are thinkers.

      AAA-1 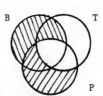 valid

17. All times when I am in trouble are times when I pray.
    All days are times when I am in trouble.
    ∴All days are times when I pray.

      AAA-1 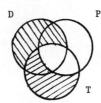 valid

71

18. All brain-processes are things in physical space.
     No after-images are things in physical space.
     ∴No after-images are brain-processes.

       AEE-2   A   B   valid

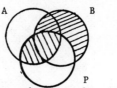

19. No simple objects are things that can be separated
         from themselves.
     All souls are simple objects.
     ∴No souls are things that can be separated from
         themselves.

       EAE-1   S   T   valid

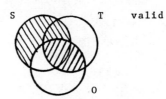

21. All practice is theory.
     All surgery is practise.
     ∴All surgery is theory.

       AAA-1   S   T   valid

22. All fightings against neighbors are evils.
     All fightings against Thebans are fightings against
         neighbors.
     ∴All fightings against Thebans are evils.

       AAA-1   T   E   valid

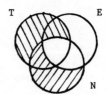

23. No things due to chance are things that reappear con-
    stantly or frequently.
    All products of Nature are things that reappear con-
    stantly or frequently.
    ∴No products of Nature are things due to chance.

EAE-2   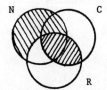   valid

24. All people to whom she speaks are ladies and gentlemen.
    No students of 9D are ladies and gentlemen.
    No students of 9D are people to whom she speaks.

AEE-2   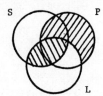   valid

26. All places where there is smoke are places where there
    is fire.
    The basement is not a place where there is smoke.
    ∴The basement is not a place where there is fire.

AEE-1   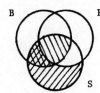   invalid
                                (Illicit
                                Major)

27. No times that Bill goes to work are times that Bill
    wears a sweater.
    This morning is a time that Bill wears a sweater.
    ∴This morning is not a time that Bill goes to work.

EAE-2   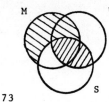   valid

73

28. All times that Cynthia compliments Henry are times that
       Henry is cheerful.
    Now is a time that Henry is cheerful.
    ∴ Now is a time that Cynthia compliments Henry.

    AAA-2

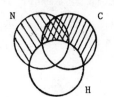

    invalid
    (Undistri-
    buted Mid-
    dle)

29. Some things that glitter are not gold.
    All things that glitter are precious metals.
    ∴ Some precious metals are not gold.

    OAO-3

    valid

31. No persons who are truly objective are persons likely
       to be mistaken.
    All persons likely to be mistaken are persons who
       ignore the facts.
    ∴ No persons who ignore the facts are persons who are
       truly objective.

    EAE-4

    invalid
    (Illicit
    Minor)

32. All excessive drinkers are debtors.
    Some excessive drinkers are not unemployed persons.
    ∴ Some unemployed persons are not debtors.

    AOO-3

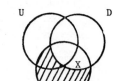

    invalid
    (Illicit
    Major)

33. All arguments worthy of logical recognition are
       arguments such as would occur in ordinary discourse.
    No arguments such as would occur in ordinary discourse
       are arguments in the fourth figure.
    ∴No arguments in the fourth figure are arguments
       worthy of logical recognition.

AEE-4   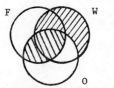   valid

34. All valid syllogisms are syllogisms that distribute
       their middle terms in at least one premiss.
    This syllogism is a syllogism that distributes its
       middle term in at least one premiss.
    ∴This syllogism is a valid syllogism.

AAA-2   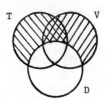   invalid
                                   (Undistri-
                                   buted Mid-
                                   dle)

36. All invalid syllogisms are syllogisms that commit an
       illicit major.
    This syllogism is not an invalid syllogism.
    ∴This syllogism is not a syllogism that commits an
       illicit major.

AEE-1   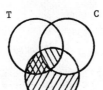   invalid
                                   (Illicit
                                   Major)

75

37. No valid syllogisms are syllogisms having two negative
    premisses.
    All syllogisms on this page are valid syllogisms.
    ∴No syllogisms on this page are syllogisms having two
    negative premisses.

       EAE-1 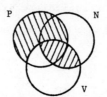 valid

38. No syllogisms having two negative premisses are valid
    syllogisms.
    Some valid syllogisms are not unsound arguments.
    ∴Some unsound arguments are syllogisms having two nega-
    tive premisses.

       EOI-4 invalid
(Exclusive
Premisses)

39. All places with vegetation are places where water is
    present.
    This place is a place with vegetation.
    ∴This place is a place where water is present.

       AAA-1 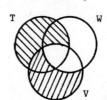 valid

41. All situations in which much money is involved are
    situations in which competition is stiff.
    This situation is a situation in which much money is
    involved.
    ∴This situation is a situation in which competition
    is stiff.

AAA-1   T   C   valid

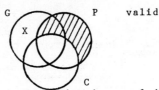

M

42. All penniless persons were convicted persons.
    Some guilty persons were not convicted persons.
    ∴ Some guilty persons were not penniless persons.

AOO-2   G   P   valid

C

43. All times when he is sick are times when he complains
    This time is not a time when he is sick.
    ∴ This time is not a time when he complains.

AEE-1   T   C   invalid
                                      (Illicit
                                      Major)

S

44. Some men are handsome creatures.
    All vile creatures are men.
    ∴ Some vile creatures are handsome creatures.

IAI-1   V   H   invalid
                                        (Undistri-
                                        buted Mid-
                                        dle)

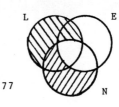

M

45. All trains not stopping at this station are trains that
    are the express train.
    The last train was a train not stopping at this station.
    ∴ The last train was a train that is the express train.

AAA-1   L   E   valid

N

46. All buildings over three hundred feet tall are sky-
    scrapers.
    Some examples of modern architecture are not sky-
    scrapers.
    ∴ Some examples of modern architecture are not buildings
    over three hundred feet tall.

AOO-2 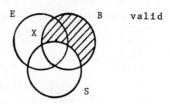 valid

Exercises on pages 243-245
    2. Second order.
        All things that are ever in motion are things that
        are immortal.
        The soul through all her being is a thing that is
        ever in motion.
        ∴ The soul through all her being is a thing that
        is immortal.

AAA-1 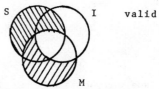 valid

    Valid second order enthymeme with missing minor
    premiss that is certainly plausible in the context
    of Plato's time.

    3. Third order.
        All persons who know the job are persons who know
        the buck.
        Abe is a person who knows the buck.
        ∴ Abe is a person who knows the job.

AAA-2 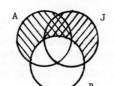 invalid
(Undistri-
buted Mid-
dle)

78

Invalid third order enthymeme: <u>no</u> syllogistic
conclusion follows validly from these premisses.
4. First order.
        All things of great worth and importance are things
            that are likely to be stolen.
        No textbooks are things that are likely to be stolen.
        ∴No textbooks are things of great worth and
            importance.

        AEE-2 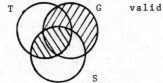 valid

        Valid first order enthymeme with plausible missing
        major premiss.
6. Third order.
        All successful people are well-groomed persons.
        Leslie Cole is a well-groomed person.

        The term common to these two premisses is not
        distributed in either of them, so no syllogistic
        conclusion follows validly from these two pre-
        misses.   Invalid enthymeme regardless of context.
7. First order.
        All persons who believe that all that exists is
            spiritual are Idealists.
        I am a person who believes that all that exists is
            spiritual.
        ∴I am an Idealist.

        AAA-1 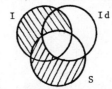 valid

        Valid first order enthymeme with true missing major
        premiss.
8. First order.
        All places that Mary went are places her lamb went.
        The opera is a place that Mary went.
        ∴The opera is a place her lamb went.

79

AAA-1 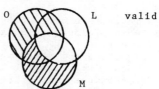 valid

Valid enthymeme whose major premiss has traditionally been expressed as: "Everywhere that Mary went her lamb was sure to go."

9. First order.
    No things before the court are appropriate subjects for discussion.
    The legal propriety of Manchester's book is a thing before the courts.
    ∴.The legal propriety of Manchester's book is not an appropriate subject for discussion.

EAE-1 valid

Valid enthymeme whose major premiss would probably be expressed as "Nothing is an appropriate subject for discussion whose legal propriety is before the courts."

11. Second order.
    All physicians are college graduates.
    All members of the A.M.A. are physicians.
    ∴.All members of the A.M.A. are college graduates.

AAA-1 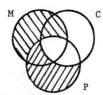 valid

Valid enthymeme with plausible missing minor premiss.

12. Third order.
    All things of which we have ideas are things of which we have experience.
    No divine attributes and operations are things of which we have experience.
    ∴.No divine attributes and operations are things of which we have ideas.

A EE-2 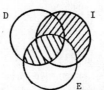 valid

Valid enthymeme whose conclusion might be more
naturally stated as "We have no ideas of divine
attributes and operations."

13. First order.
      All times following rain are times fish do not bite.
      This time is a time fish do not bite.
      ∴This time is a time following rain.

AAA-2 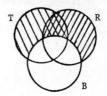 invalid
(Undistri-
buted Mid-
dle)

Invalid enthymeme if the plausible premiss "Fish
never bite after a rain" is understood. It is
valid, however, if the suppressed premiss is the
unplausible "Only after a rain do fish fail to
bite."

14. Third order.
      All men having a lean and hungry look are dangerous
        men.
      Yond Cassius is a man having a lean and hungry look.
      ∴Yond Cassius is a dangerous man.

AAA-1 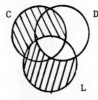 valid

16. First order.
      All persons who have telephones are persons whose
        names are listed in the phone book.
      Adamson is not a person whose name is listed in the
        phone book.
      ∴Adamson is not a person who has a telephone.

AEE-2 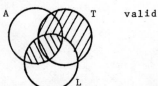 valid

Valid enthymeme if the understood major premiss is the (moderately) plausible "No one whose name is not listed in the phone book has a telephone. On the other hand, if the understood premiss is the (somewhat) more plausible "Everyone whose name is listed in the phone book has a telephone," then the enthymeme is invalid:

    All persons whose names are listed in the phone book are persons who have telephones.
    Adamsom is not a person whose name is listed in the phone book.
    ∴Adamson is not a person who has a telephone.

AEE-1 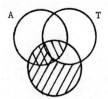 invalid
(Illicit
Major)

17. Second order.
    No enthymemes are complete arguments.
    This argument is an enthymeme.
    ∴This argument is not a complete argument.

EAE-1 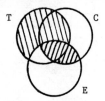 valid

    Sound enthymeme since the missing minor premiss is obviously true.
18. First order.
    All ambitious persons are persons who would take the
      crown.
    He is not a person who would take the crown.
    ∴He is not an ambitious person.

AEE-2 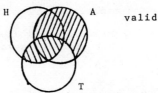 valid

Valid enthymeme if the understood major premiss
is the questionable premiss "Any ambitious person
would take the crown."
But if the suppressed premiss is the more plausible
"Anyone who would take the crown must be ambitious,"
then the enthymeme is invalid:

    All persons who would take the crown are
    ambitious persons.
    He is not a person who would take the crown.
    ∴He is not an ambitious person.

AEE-1 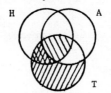 invalid
(Illicit
Major)

19. First order.

    All difficult arguments are arguments completed
       only by good students.
    This argument is a difficult argument.
    ∴This argument is an argument completed only by
    good students.

AAA-1 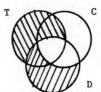 valid

Valid enthymeme which may alternatively be com-
pleted:

    All readers who complete a difficult argument
    are good students.
    All readers who complete this argument are
    readers who complete a difficult argument.
    ∴All readers who complete this argument are
    good students.
    AAA-1

21. Third order.
        No sense knowledge is immaterial knowledge.
        Some immaterial knowledge is knowledge we possess.
        ∴Some knowledge we possess is not sense knowledge.

        EIO-4   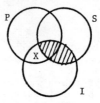   valid

22. Third order.
        All taxes laid specifically on the exercise of
          these freedoms are unconstitutional taxes.
        The license tax imposed by this ordinance is a
          tax laid specifically on the exercise of
          these freedoms.
        ∴.The license tax imposed by this ordinance is an
          unconstitutional tax.

        AAA-1   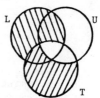   valid

        Valid enthymeme whose conclusion would probably
        be expressed as: "This ordinance is uncon-
        stitutional."
23. Third order.
        No sinner is one who should cast the first stone.
        All persons here are sinners.
        ∴.No person here is one who should cast the first
          stone.

        EAE-1   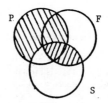   valid

        Valid enthymeme whose conclusion would probably be
        expressed as: "No one here,should criticize me."

24. Third order.
No demonstrative proofs that there was no Creation
are things that exist in Nature.
All things that should be able to make you abandon
the theory of the Creation are demonstrative
proofs that there was no Creation.
∴No things that should be able to make you abandon
the theory of the Creation are things that exist
in Nature.

EAE-1 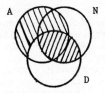 valid

26. First order.
All species that tend to increase at a greater
rate than their means of subsistence are species
that are occasionally subject to a severe
struggle for existence.
Man is a species that tends to increase at a
greater rate than their means of subsistence.
∴Man is a species that is occasionally subject to
a severe struggle for existence.

AAA-1 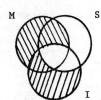 valid

27. Third order.
No internal combustion engines are pollution-free
devices.
No internal combustion engines are completely
efficient machines.

EE?-3   Both premises are negative so no
syllogistic conclusion follows validly
from them. Invalid enthymeme regardless of context.

28. Third order.
All nations without souls are nations that cannot
live.
All nations without consciences are nations without
souls.

85

∴All nations without consciences are nations that cannot live.

AAA-1 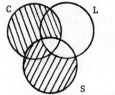 valid

Valid enthymeme whose conclusion would probably be expressed as "A nation without a conscience (is a nation that?) cannot live."

29. First order.

All responsibilities are things dreaded by most men.
All liberties are responsibilities.
∴All liberties are things dreaded by most men.

AAA-1 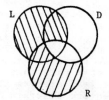 valid

If this passage is an argument then it is a valid enthymeme whose major premiss would probably be expressed as "Most men dread responsibility." It may not express an argument at all, but rather an explanation of why most men dread liberty (see Section 1.4).

30. Second order.

All times in which the theatre could exist are times when it is possible to pretend to motives and abilities other than one's real ones, or to pretend to strengths of motives and levels of ability other than their real strengths and levels.
All times are times in which the theatre could exist.
∴All times are times when it is possible to pretend, etc.

AAA-1 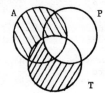 valid

86

<u>Exercises on pages 247-249</u>
I. 2. (1') All experienced persons are competent persons.
        (3') No competent persons are persons who are always
             blundering.
        (2') Jenkins is a person who is always blundering.
        ∴Jenkins is not an experienced person.

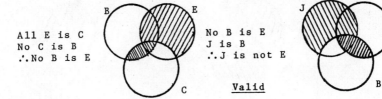

All E is C   No B is E
No C is B   J is B
∴No B is E   ∴J is not E   <u>Valid</u>

3. (3') All romances in this library are books in this
         library that are healthy in tone.
    (1') All books in this library that are healthy in tone
         are books in this library that I recommend for
         reading.
    (4') All books in this library that I recommend for
         reading are bound books in this library.
    (2') All bound books in this library are well-written
         books.
    ∴All romances in this library are well-written books.

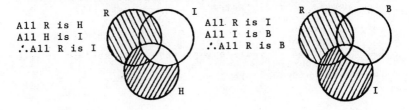

All R is H   All R is I
All H is I   All I is B
∴All R is I   ∴All R is B

87

All R is B
All B is W
∴All R is W

Valid

4. (1') All Oxford dons are profound scholars.
(4') All profound scholars are great lovers of music.
(2') No insensitive souls are great lovers of music.
(3') No insensitive souls are Don Juans.
∴All Oxford dons are Don Juans.

All O is P
All P is G
∴All O is G

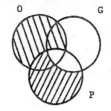

All O is G
No I is G
∴No O is I

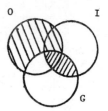

No O is I
No I is D
∴All O is D

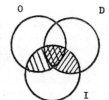

Invalid

5. (1') All interesting poems are poems that are popular
among people of real taste.
(4') No affected poems are poems that are popular among
people of real taste.
(2') All modern poems are affected poems.
(5') All poems on the subject of soap bubbles are
modern poems.
(3') All poems of yours are poems on the subject of
soap bubbles.
∴No poems of yours are interesting poems.

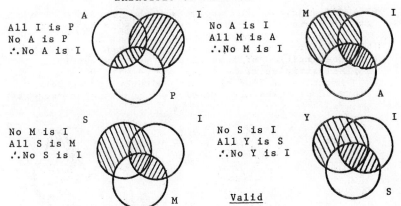

All I is P
No A is P
∴No A is I

No A is I
All M is A
∴No M is I

No M is I
All S is M
∴No S is I

No S is I
All Y is S
∴No Y is I   Valid

6. (3') All contributors to the new magazine are poets.
   (1') All poets are writers.
   (4') No military officers are writers.
   (2') All astronauts are military officers.
   ∴No astronauts are contributors to the new magazine.

All P are W
All C are P
∴All C are W

All C are W
No M are W
∴No M are C

No M are C
All A are M
∴No A are C   Valid

II. 2. (2') This dish is a pudding.
       (1') All puddings are nice things.
       (3') No nice things are wholesome things.
       ∴This dish is not a wholesome thing.

D is P
All P is N
∴D is N

D is N
No N is W
∴D is not W   Valid

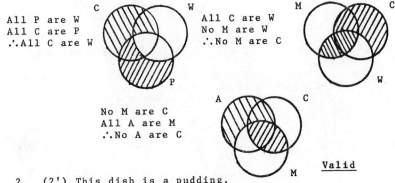

89

3. (3') All wedding cakes are very rich articles of food.
    (1') No articles of food allowed me by my doctor are
         very rich articles of food.
    (4') All articles of food that are suitable for supper
         are articles of food allowed me by my doctor.
    (2') All articles of food that agree with me are
         articles of food that are suitable for supper.
    ∴No wedding cakes are articles of food that agree with
      me.

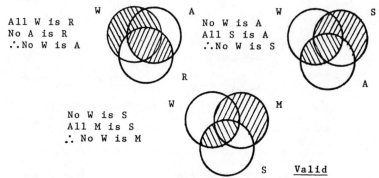

```
All W is R                No W is A
No A is R                 All S is A
∴No W is A                ∴No W is S
```

```
No W is S
All M is S
∴ No W is M
```
Valid

4. (3') All gluttons, who are children of mine, are fat
         persons.
    (1') No sons of mine are fat persons.
    (4') All children of mine who take exercise are sons
         of mine.
    (2') All children of mine who are healthy are children
         of mine who take exercise.
    ∴No children of mine who are healthy are gluttons.

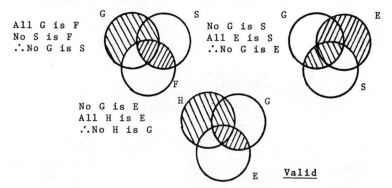

```
All G is F                No G is S
No S is F                 All E is S
∴No G is S                ∴No G is E
```

```
No G is E
All H is E
∴No H is G
```
Valid

90

5. (2') These Sorites are examples not arranged in regular
   order, like the examples I am used to.
   (4') No examples not arranged in regular order, like
   the examples I am used to, are examples I can
   understand.
   (1') All examples I do not grumble at are examples I
   can understand.
   (5') All examples that do not give me a headache are
   examples I do not grumble at.
   (3') All easy examples are examples that do not give me
   a headache.
   ∴ These Sorites are not easy examples.

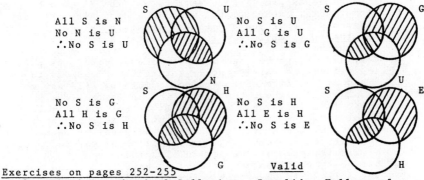

All S is N   No S is U
No N is U   All G is U
∴ No S is U   ∴ No S is G

No S is G   No S is H
All H is G   All E is H
∴ No S is H   ∴ No S is E

                    Valid

Exercises on pages 252-255
2. Mixed Hypothetical Syllogism. Invalid: Fallacy of
Affirming the Consequent. 3. Pure Hypothetical Syllogism.
Valid. 4. Mixed Hypothetical Syllogism. Modus Ponens.
Valid. 6. Mixed Hypothetical Syllogism. Modus Tollens.
Valid. 7. Mixed Hypothetical Syllogism. Invalid: Fallacy
of Denying the Antecedent. 8. Disjunctive Syllogism.
Invalid. 9. Mixed Hypothetical Syllogism. Modus Tollens.
Valid. 11. Mixed Hypothetical Syllogism. Invalid: Fallacy
of Denying the Antecedent. 12. Mixed Hypothetical Syllogism.
Modus Ponens. Valid. 13. Mixed Hypothetical Syllogism.
Invalid: Fallacy of Affirming the Consequent. 14. Disjunctive Syllogism, formally invalid as it stands. Dis-
carding the stated disjunctive premiss, however, gives us a
valid enthymeme with the unexpressed premiss being the true
proposition Either Mr. Robinson does not live in Detroit
or Mr. Robinson does not live in Chicago. 16. Mixed
Hypothetical Syllogism. Modus Tollens. Valid. 17. Disjunctive Syllogism. Valid. 18. Mixed Hypothetical
Syllogism. Modus Tollens. Valid. 19. Disjunctive Syllogism. Valid. 21. Disjunctive Syllogism. Valid. 22.
Mixed Hypothetical Syllogism. Invalid: Fallacy of Denying
the Antecedent. 23. Mixed Hypothetical Syllogism. Modus

Tollens. Valid. 24. Mixed Hypothetical Syllogism.
Modus Tollens. Valid. 26. Mixed Hypothetical
Syllogism. Modus Tollens. Valid. 27. Mixed Hypo-
thetical Syllogism. Modus Tollens. Valid. 28. Mixed
Hypothetical Syllogism. Modus Tollens. 29. Pure
Hypothetical Syllogism. Valid. 30. Mixed Hypothetical
Syllogism. Modus Tollens. Valid.

Exercises on pages 259-262

2. Impossible to go between the horns. Plausible to grasp
by either horn. Rebuttal plausible but not a refutation.

3. Perhaps possible to go between the horns in that we may
partially understand something - at least enough for it
to be intelligible without its being already understood.
This suggests plausible ways to grasp the dilemma by
either horn. Rebuttal not plausible here, for the conclusion whatever you say either enlarges my understanding
or else is intelligible to me is not particularly
attractive.

4. Very easy to go between the horns here (since the preceding dilemma is fairly easily refuted). Plausible to
grasp by the first horn - since something said may well
be of value without "enlarging the understanding,"
which is a very vague notion. It is not possible to
rebut a simple constructive dilemma of this ordinary
type using the ingredients of the original argument.
However, other rebutting counter-dilemmas can be thought
of easily, some of them quite plausible.

6. Very easy to go between the horns here (since the preceding dilemma is so easily refuted). Plausible to grasp
by the second horn - since a deductive argument that
establishes a familiar conclusion may well be of some
value ("bringing nothing new to light" is again an
ambiguous phrase). No rebuttal can be made of the
original dilemma's ingredients, but other rebutting
counter-dilemmas can be thought of easily.

7. Very easy to go between the horns here. Plausible to
grasp by either horn. A nonrefuting rebuttal can be
made here, but it is not very plausible.

8. Very easy to go between the horns here. Grasping by
the horns may or may not be plausible - a debatable
point, perhaps. No rebuttal using the original dilemma's
ingredients, but other rebutting counter-dilemmas can
be thought of easily.

9. Perhaps possible to go between the horns in that going
to war and stopping soon after U.N. action and threat
of intervention may be a third and distinct possibility.
Very plausible to grasp by either horn (the second if
we note that "unsuccessful in its purpose of preventing
war" in the premiss has become simply "unsuccessful"
in the conclusion) since the U.N. may be necessary for

purposes other than keeping peace and may be successful
in realizing those other purposes. The usual plausible
but nonrefuting rebuttal can be constructed out of the
original dilemma's ingredients.

11.   Perhaps possible to go between the horns if there is or
can be a mode of living somewhere between extravagant and
modest. Plausible to grasp by either horn: one who
lives extravagantly has no money left to contribute; one
who lives modestly does so because he has no money for
either extravagances or contributions. The usual
plausible but nonrefuting rebuttal can be constructed
out of the original dilemma's ingredients.

12.   This argument, as stated, is not very persuasive. The
leap to the explicit conclusion is clearly wild, being an
ignoratio elenchus. But there is a highly enthymematic
dilemma present, with only its conjunctive premiss stated.
The suppressed disjunctive premiss may be understood to
to assert of every thing that a man either knows it or
does not know it. And the understood conclusion asserts
of every thing that either a man has no need to enquire
about it or cannot enquire about it. It is perhaps
possible to go between the horns in that we may have
partial knowledge of a thing: enough to know the subject
but not well enough to have no need to enquire further.
This suggests plausible ways to grasp the dilemma by
either horn. Rebuttal not plausible here, for the conclusion that either a man has need to enquire about a
thing or else he can enquire about that thing is not
particularly attractive.

13.   This dilemma is enthymematic, with the suppressed disjunctive premiss understood to assert that you must
either not resist (lie still) or resist iniquitous
power. The strictly dilemmatic conclusion is also understood: you are either considered as an accomplice in
iniquitous measures or you are accused of provoking
irritable power to new excesses. It is of course impossible to go between the horns here, if "lying still"
is taken to be the same as "not resisting." But if these
are distinguished, one might attempt to argue that
there is a middle ground of voicing opposition without
forcibly resisting. This suggests a plausible way to
grasp the dilemma by its first horn. The usual nonrefuting rebuttal can be constructed here, but it does
not seem very attractive.

14.   Another enthymematic dilemma with disjunctive premiss
suppressed. Impossible to go between the horns here.
Either horn can be grasped easily and successfully, I
believe, by distinguishing between what a thing is,
in the sense of properties that may be predicated of
it, and what a thing is, in the sense of what it is

identical to. The argument can be regarded as committing the fallacy of equivocation.

16. Easy to go between the horns here: a thing moves <u>from</u> the place where it is <u>to</u> a place where it is not. It is plausible to grasp by the first horn by observing that a rotating object moves in the place where it is <u>while</u> remaining therein. One might grasp the second horn by rejecting (with Whitehead) simple location as a fallacy, and maintaining that everything is everywhere--in the sense of influencing what happens there. It is hard to see what kind of rebuttal might be available here.

17. Plausible to go between the horns here, and either request or entreat the young men not to flock to him, or (somehow) arrange with their elders to keep them away. One might grasp the first horn and argue that young men do not have enough influence on their elders to cause them to drive someone out of the city "on request." It is not so easy to grasp the second horn because that is what happened in Athens itself. The usual plausible but nonrefuting rebuttal can be constructed out of the original dilemma's ingredients.

18. Plausible to go between the horns here and say that Socrates' dying was the boundary between the time he was alive and the time he was dead. Perhaps one might grasp the first horn and insist that when the act of dying was finished the living was finished too. It is hard to construct any plausible rebuttal here.

19. Of the first dilemma one must admit that as it is formulated here one cannot go between the horns, at least if "more than a synonym" is understood as "other than a synonym." But grasping the first horn is easy, especially along Fregean lines which distinguish sense from reference. And grasping the second horn is also possible, with one plausible move turning on equivocations that need untangling, another turning on the legitimate aim of improving the terms (or concepts) being analysed. The usual nonrefuting rebuttal can be constructed out of the original dilemma's ingredients. Of the second dilemma, one can go between the horns by remarking on the fact that directions for the proper use of a new term need not take the form of, or be reducible to, an explicit definition of it. This suggests a plausible way of grasping the first horn. The usual nonrefuting rebuttal can be constructed out of the original dilemma's ingredients.

20. Very easy to go between the horns here. A non-Muslim would be willing to grasp the second horn. The usual nonrefuting rebuttal can be constructed out of the original dilemma's ingredients.

21. The horns can be gone between here, because there is a continuum stretching from <u>mere</u> duplication of the ideas

through reporting of those ideas plus amplification, supplementation, pointing out their consequences and implications, and contrasting them with alternatives; and starting from the other horn one can increasingly amend, clarify, remove ambiguities and vagueness from the original formulation. Either horn can be grasped: one can deviate from the formulation by clarifying, removing clearly accidental ambiguities and unintended vagueness without being unjust; one can duplicate the ideas and then go on to amplify and explain the consequences of the ideas of the thinker being interpreted and thus make the interpretation valuable. And the usual nonrefuting rebuttal can be constructed out of the original dilemma's ingredients.

22. There were in theory a number of ways to go between the horns here: between defiance and obedience to the Court decision there are many degrees of partial compliance short of full obedience yet not outright full defiance either. Either horn could be grasped--at least in theory: an emergency situation in the international sphere might prevent defiance from being followed by impeachment; and it was logically possible that the evidence produced by obedience to the order might not have been sufficient to persuade the Congress to impeach. A nonrefuting rebuttal is barely possible, but not very persuasive or helpful (if he defied the order he would not "be impeached on the evidence," and if he obeyed the order he would not be impeached for defiance--but he would still have been impeached for one or the other.)

Exercises on pages 274-277

I. 2. T 3. F 4. F 6. T 7. F 8. T 9. F 11. F 12. T
13. F 14. F 16. T 17. T 18. F 19. T 21. F 22. T
23. F 24. T 25. F

II. 2. F 3. T 4. T 6. T 7. T 8. F 9. T 11. T 12. F
13. F 14. F 16. T 17. F 18. F 19. T 21. F 22. T
23. F 24. T 25. F

III. 2. F 3. T 4. F 6. T 7. F 8. F 9. T 11. F 12. F
13. T 14. T 16. T 17. T 18. F 19. F 21. F 22. F
23. F 24. T 25. F

IV. 2. I v L 3. I·L 4. ~(I·L) 6. (I v L)·~(I·L)
7. S·(I v J) 8. (S·I) v J 9. ~E·J 11. ~E v J
12. ~(E·J) 13. J v S 14. E v L 16. (I·L) v (~I·~L)
17. L·E 18. ~(~I·~L) 19. (E·J) v (~I·~L) 21. (E·S) v
(J v L) 22. S·[J v (L·I)] 23. (E v J)·(~L·~I)
24. E·(S·L) 25. (L·E)·(S·J)

Exercises on pages 285-288

I. 2. F 3. F 4. T 6. F 7. T 8. T 9. F 11. F 12. F
13. T 14. T 16. T 17. F 18. F 19. T 21. T 22. F
23. F 24. F 25. T

II. 2. T 3. F 4. T 6. F 7. T 8. T 9. F 11. T
12. F 13. F 14. T 16. T 17. F 18. F 19. T
21. T 22. F 23. T 24. F 25. T

III. 2. A ⊃ (B v C) 3. A ⊃ (B·C) 4. (A ⊃ B)·C
6. (A v B) ⊃ C 7. A v (B ⊃ C) 8. ~A ⊃ (~B v ~C)
9. ~A ⊃ (~B·~C) 11. (~A ⊃ ~B)·C 12. A ⊃ B
13. B ⊃ A 14. C ⊃ (A·B) 16. (B v C) ⊃ A 17. B v C
18. A ⊃ (B v C) 19. ~B v A 21. A ⊃ B
22. C ⊃ A 23. (A·B) ⊃ (C·D) 24. (A·B) ⊃ (C v D)
25. (~C·~D) ⊃ (~B v A)

Exercises on pages 297-299

I. b. 6 is the specific form of b.
c. 4 is the specific form of c.
d. 9 is the specific form of d.
f. 16 is the specific form of f.
g. 8 is the specific form of g.
h. 11 is the specific form of h.
i. 12 is the specific form of i.
k. 4 has k as a substitution instance.
l. 3 has l as a substitution instance.
m. 3 has m as a substitution instance, and 24 also has m as a substitution instance.
n. 8 has n as a substitution instance, and 21 is the specific form of n.
o. 3 has o as a substitution instance, and 24 is the specific form of o.

II. 2. Invalid - shown by row 3. 3. Valid. 4. Valid 6. Valid
7. Valid 8. Invalid - shown by row 3. 9. Valid 11.
Invalid - shown by row 8 12. Invalid - shown by rows 5 and 7. 13. Valid 14. Valid 16. Valid 17. Valid
18. Invalid - shown by rows 6 and 8. 19. Valid 21.
Valid 22. Valid 23. Valid 24. Valid

III. 2. specific form: (p v q) ⊃ (p·q)   Valid
p·q
∴ p v q
3. specific form: p ⊃ q   Invalid - shown
q ⊃ p   by row 4.
∴ p v q
4. specific form: (p v q) ⊃ (p·q) Valid
~(p·q)
∴ ~(p v q)
6. specific form: p v q   Invalid - shown
p   by row 1.
∴ ~ q
7. specific form: p v (q·~q)   Valid
p
∴ ~(q·~q)
8. specific form: (p v q) ⊃ r   Valid
r ⊃ (p·q)
∴ (p v q) ⊃ (p·q)

96

9. specific form: (p v q) ⊃ r   Valid
r ⊃ (p·q)
∴ (p·q) ⊃ (p v q)

10. specific form: p ⊃ (q v r)   Invalid - shown
(q·r) ⊃ ~p   by rows 2 and 3.
∴ ~p

IV. 2. D ⊃ (E ⊃ F)   p ⊃ (q ⊃ r)   Valid
E   q
∴ D ⊃ F   ∴ p ⊃ r

3. G ⊃ H   p ⊃ q   Invalid-shown
G ⊃ I   p ⊃ r   by row 6
∴ H ⊃ I   ∴ q ⊃ r

4. J ⊃ (K v L)   p ⊃ (q v r)   Valid
~K   ~q
∴ J ⊃ L   ∴ p ⊃ r

6. E ⊃ P   p ⊃ q   Valid
P ⊃ S   q ⊃ r
S ⊃ ~E   r ⊃ ~p
∴ ~E   ∴ ~p

7. T ⊃ L   p ⊃ q   Valid
~T ⊃ I   ~p ⊃ r
∴ L v I   ∴ q v r

8. R ⊃ (P v D)   p ⊃ (q v r)   Valid
~P   ~q
∴~D ⊃ ~R   ∴ ~r ⊃ ~p

9. C ⊃ (I v D)   p ⊃ (q v r)   Invalid - shown
(I·D) ⊃ B   (q·r) ⊃ s   by rows 4, 6
∴ C ⊃ B   ∴ p ⊃ s

10. C ⊃ (I·D)   p ⊃ (q·r)   Valid
(I v D) ⊃ B (q v r) ⊃ s
∴ C ⊃ B   ∴ p ⊃ s

Exercises on pages 304-305

I. 2. a has 2 as a substitution instance, and d is the specific form of 2.
3. b has 3 as a substitution instance.
4. b has 4 as a substitution instance.
6. b has 6 as a substitution instance.
7. c has 7 as a substitution instance, and f has 7 as a substitution instance.
8. b has 8 as a substitution instance, and j has 8 as a substitution instance.
9. b has 9 as a substitution instance, and g has 9 as a substitution instance, and h is the specific form of 9.
10. e has 10 as a substitution instance.

II. 2. tautologous - final column TTTT 3. Self-contradictory - final column FFFF 4. Tautologous - final column TTTT 6. Self-contradictory - final column FFFF 7. Tautologous - final column TTTTTTTT 8. Self-contradictory - final column FFFFFFFF 9. Tautologous - final column TTTTTTTTTTTTTTTT 10. Contingent - final

97

EXERCISES ON PAGES 304-315

column TTTTTTTTTTFFTTFT

III. 2. Not - final column TFFT   3. Not - final column
TTTFTFTT   4. Logical Equivalence - final column TTTTTTTT
6. Logical Equivalence - final column TTTT   7. Not -
final column TFTT   8. Logical Equivalence - final column
TTTT   9. Not - final column TTFF   11. Logical Equivalence - final column TTTT   12. Not - final column FFTT
13. Logical Equivalence - final column TTTT   14. Not -
final column TTFF   16. Not - final column TTTFFTTT
17. Not - final column TTTFFTTT   18. Logical Equivalence -
final column TTTTTTT   19. Logical Equivalence - final
column TTTTTTT   20. Logical Equivalence - final column
TTTT

Exercises on pages 312-318

I. 2. Simplification (Simp.)   3. Addition (Add.)   4. Simplification (Simp.)   6. Disjunctive Syllogism (D.S.)
7. Modus Tollens (M.T.)   8. Modus Ponens (M.P.)   9.
Hypothetical Syllogism (H.S.)   11. Conjunction (Conj.)
12. Conjunction (Conj.)   13. Absorption (Abs.)   14.
Addition (Add.)   16. Disjunctive Syllogism (D.S.)   17.
Constructive Dilemma (C.D.)   18. Modus Tollens (M.T.)
19. Modus Ponens (M.P.)   20. Hypothetical Syllogism
(H.S.)

II. 2.   4. 1, Simp.
         5. 2, 4, C.D.
         6. 5, 3, D.S.
    4.   4. 1, Abs.
         5. 4, 2, M.P.
         6. 5, Abs.
         7. 6, 3, M.T.
    7.   4. 3, Simp.
         5. 4, Add.
         6. 1, 5, M.P.
         7. 6, Add.
         8. 2, 7, M.P.
         9. 8, 4, M.P.
    9.   5. 1, Abs.
         6. 5, 4, M.T.
         7. 2, 6, D.S.
         8. 7, Simp.
         9. 3, 8, M.T.
        10. 9, Add.

    3.   5. 1, 2, H.S.
         6. 5, 3, Conj.
         7. 6, 4, C.D.
    6.   5. 1, Abs.
         6. 5, 3, H.S.
         7. 2, 6, M.P.
         8. 7, 4, D.S.
    8.   5, 4, Add.
         6. 3, 5, M.P.
         7. 1, 6, M.T.
         8. 2, 7, M.P.
         9. 8, 6, M.T.
   10.   6. 4, 5, Conj.
         7. 3, 6, M.P.
         8. 7, 1, H.S.
         9. 2, 8, Conj.
        10. 9, 4, C.D.

III. 2. 1. D ⊃ E
        2. ~(D·E) / ∴ ~D
        3. D ⊃ (D·E) 1, Abs.
        4. ~D   3, 2, M.T.
     3. 1. (F v G) ⊃ H
        2. F   / ∴ H
        3. F v G   2, Add
        4. H   1, 3, M.P.

98

```
  4.  1. I ⊃ J
      2. (I·J) ⊃ K  /  ∴  I ⊃ K
      3. I ⊃ (I·J)        1, Abs.
      4. I ⊃ K            3, 2, H.S.
  6.  1. (O v P) ⊃ Q
      2. ~Q·~O        /  ∴  ~(O v P)
      3. ~Q               2, Simp.
      4. ~(O v P)         1, 3, M.T.
  7.  1. R ⊃ S
      2. R v T
      3. T ⊃ U    /  ∴  S v U
      4. (R ⊃ S)·(T ⊃ U)  1, 3, Conj.
      5. S v U            4, 2, C.D.
  8.  1. (V·W) v (X ⊃ Y)
      2. Z ⊃ X
      3. ~(V·W)   /  ∴  Z ⊃ Y
      4. X ⊃ Y            1, 3, D.S.
      5. Z ⊃ Y            2, 4, H.S.
  9.  1. (A ⊃ B)·(C ⊃ D)
      2. B ⊃ D
      3. (B ⊃ D) ⊃ (A v C)/ ∴ B v D
      4. A v C            3, 2, M.P.
      5. B v D            1, 4, C.D.
 10.  1. E v ~F
      2. F ⊃ ~G
      3. ~E       / ∴ (F ⊃ ~G)·~F
      4. ~F              1, 3, D.S.
      5. (F ⊃ ~G)·~F     2, 4, Conj.
IV. 2. 1. D ⊃ E
      2. F v ~E
      3. ~F·~D   / ∴ ~D
      4. ~F              3, Simp.
      5. ~E              2, 4, D.S.
      6. ~D              1, 5, M.T.
    3. 1. G ⊃ H
      2. I ⊃ J
      3. G v I   / ∴ (H v J) v I
      4. (G ⊃ H)·(I ⊃ J) 1, 2, Conj.
      5. H v J           4, 3, C.D.
      6. (H v J) v I     5, Add.
    4. 1. (K v L) ⊃ (M v N)
      2. (M v N) ⊃ (O·P)
      3. K       /∴ O
      4. K v L           3, Add.
      5. M v N           1, 4, M.P.
      6. O·P             2, 5, M.P.
      7. O               6, Simp.
    6. 1. W ⊃ X
      2. (W·X) ⊃ Y
      3. (W·Y) ⊃ Z /∴ W ⊃ Z
```

```
        4. W  ⊃ (W·X)                              1, Abs.
        5. W  ⊃ Y                                  4, 2, H.S.
        6. W  ⊃ (W·Y)                              5, Abs.
        7. W  ⊃ Z                                  6, 3, H.S.
   7. 1. A  ⊃ B
      2. C  ⊃ D
      3. A v C              /∴  (A·B) v (C·D)
      4. A  ⊃ (A·B)                               1, Abs.
      5. C  ⊃ (C·D)                               2, Abs.
      6. [A  ⊃ (A·B)]·[C  ⊃ (C·D)]                4, 5, Conj.
      7. (A·B) v (C·D)                            6, 3, C.D.
   8. 1. (E v F) ⊃ (G·H)
      2. (G v H) ⊃  I
      3. E               /∴  I
      4. E v F                                    3, Add.
      5. G·H                                      1, 4, M.P.
      6. G                                        5, Simp.
      7. G v H                                    6, Add.
      8. I                                        2, 7, M.P.
   9. 1. J  ⊃ K
      2. K v L
      3. (L·~J)  ⊃ (M·~J)
      4. ~K              /∴  M
      5. L                                        2, 4, D.S.
      6. ~J                                       1, 4, M.T.
      7. L·~J                                     5, 6, Conj.
      8. M·~J                                     3, 7, M.P.
      9. M                                        8, Simp.
  10. 1. (N v O) ⊃ P
      2. (P v Q) ⊃ R
      3. Q v N
      4. ~Q                  /∴  R
      5. N                                        3, 4, D.S.
      6. N v O                                    5, Add.
      7. P                                        1, 6, M.P.
      8. P v Q                                    7, Add.
      9. R                                        2, 8, M.P.
V.   2. 1. (A ⊃ S)·(B ⊃ F)
        2. A v B
        3. (S ⊃ B)·(F ⊃ W)   /∴  B v W
        4. S v F                                  1, 2, C.D.
        5. B v W                                  3, 4, C.D.
     3. 1. (R ⊃ P)·(P ⊃ ~L)
        2. T ⊃ L
        3. R v T               /∴  P v L
        4. R ⊃ P                                  1, Simp.
        5. (R ⊃ P)·(T ⊃ L)                        4, 2, Conj.
        6. P v L                                  5, 3, C.D.
     4. 1. (N ⊃ O)·(P ⊃ Q)
        2. (R ⊃ S)·(S ⊃ T)
        3. N v R               /∴  O v S
```

100

      4. N ⊃ O   1, Simp.
      5. R ⊃ S   2, Simp.
      6. (N ⊃ O)·(R ⊃ S)   4, 5, Conj.
      7. O v S   6, 3, C.D.
  6. 1. (J ⊃ R)·(~J ⊃ E)
      2. R ⊃ I
      3. [(J ⊃ R)·(R ⊃ I)] ⊃ [(J·I) v (~J·~I)]
      4. (J·I) ⊃ T
      5. (~J·~I) ⊃ D   /∴ T v D
      6. J ⊃ R   1, Simp.
      7. (J ⊃ R)·(R ⊃ I)   6, 2, Conj.
      8. (J·I) v (~J·~I)   3, 7, M.P.
      9. [(J·I) ⊃ T]·[(~J·~I) ⊃ D]   4, 5, Conj.
     10. T v D   9, 8, C.D.
  7. 1. A ⊃ B
      2. (A·B) ⊃ (C v D)
      3. (C v D) ⊃ ~E
      4. (A ⊃ ~E) ⊃ F   /∴F
      5. A ⊃ (A·B)   1, Abs.
      6. A ⊃ (C v D)   5, 2, H.S.
      7. A ⊃ ~E   6, 3, H.S.
      8. F   4, 7, M.P.
  8. 1. J ⊃ E
      2. E ⊃ T
      3. ~T
      4. R ⊃ H
      5. D ⊃ ~H
      6. D
      7. ~J ⊃ (R v S)   /∴ S
      8. J ⊃ T   1, 2, H.S.
      9. ~J   8, 3, M.T.
     10. R v S   7, 9, M.P.
     11. ~H   5, 6, M.P.
     12. ~R   4, 11, M.T.
     13. S   10, 12, D.S.
  9. 1. S ⊃ W
      2. W ⊃ ~L
      3. S
      4. D ⊃ ~I
      5. D
      6. L v (I v C)
      7. C ⊃ B   /∴ B
      8. W   1, 3, M.P.
      9. ~L   2, 8, M.P.
     10. I v C   6, 9, D.S.
     11. ~I   4, 5, M.P.
     12. C   10, 11, D.S.
     13. B   7, 12, M.P.
 10. 1. O ⊃ ~M
      2. O
      3. B ⊃ ~N
      4. B
                       101

EXERCISES ON PAGES 318-326

```
 5. (~M·~N) ⊃ F
 6. (B·F) ⊃ G          /∴ G
 7. ~M                           1, 2, M.P.
 8. ~N                           3, 4, M.P.
 9. ~M·~N                        7, 8, Conj.
10. F                           5, 9, M.P.
11. B·F                         4, 10, Conj.
12. G                           6, 11, M.P.
```

Exercises on pages 323-330

I. 2. Material Implication (Impl.) 3. Exportation (Exp.)
    4. Tautology (Taut.) 6. De Morgan's Theorem (De M.)
    7. Exportation (Exp.) 8. Distribution (Dist.) 9.
    Double Negation (D.N.) 11. Material Implication
    (Impl.) 12. Transposition (Trans.) 13. De Morgan's
    Theorem (De M.) 14. Association (Assoc.) 16. Tauto-
    logy (Taut.) 17. Material Equivalence (Equiv.)
    18. Double Negation (D.N.) 19. Distribution (Dist.)
    20. De Morgan's Theorem (De M.)

```
II.  2. 3. 1, Com.              3. 3. 2, Add.
        4. 3, Exp.                 4. 3, Com.
        5. 4, 2, H.S.              5. 1, 4, M.P.
                                   6. 5, Assoc.
                                   7. 6, Simp.
     4. 3, 2. Add.              6. 4. 2, Exp.
        4. 3, De M.                5. 3, De M.
        5. 1, 4, M.T.              6. 4, 5, Conj.
        6. 5, De M.                7. 1, Dist.
        7. 6, Simp.                8. 6, 7, C.D.
                                   9. 8, Equiv.
     7. 5. 3, Equiv.           8. 5. 1, 2, H.S.
        6. 5, 4, D.S.             6. 5, 3, Conj.
        7. 6, De M.                7. 6, Equiv.
        8. 1, 2, H.S.              8. 7, Equiv.
        9. 8, Exp.                 9. 4, Impl.
       10. 9, Taut.              10. 9, De M.
       11. 10, 7, M.T.          11. 8, 10, D.S.
     9. 4. 3, Equiv.          10.    3. 2, Trans.
        5. 4, Simp.                  4. 3, Exp.
        6. 5, Abs.                   5. 1, D.N.
        7. 6, 1. H.S.                6. 5, Com.
        8. 2, Dist.                  7. 6, Dist.
        9. 8, Simp.                  8. 7, Com.
       10. 9, D.N.                   9. 4, 8, C.D.
       11. 10, Impl.                10. 9, Com.
       12. 7, 11, H.S.             11. 10, D.N.
                                   12. 11, De M.

III. 2. 1. C              /∴  D ⊃ C
        2. C v ~D
        3. ~D v C                     1, Add.
        4. D ⊃ G                      2, Com.
                                      3, Impl.
```

```
 3.  1. E ⊃ (F ⊃ G)      /∴ F ⊃ (E ⊃ G)
     2. (E·F) ⊃ G                          1, Exp.
     3. (F·E) ⊃ G                          2, Com.
     4. F ⊃ (E ⊃ G)                        3, Exp.
 4.  1. H ⊃ (I·J)         /∴ H ⊃ I
     2. ~H v (I·J)                         1, Impl.
     3. (~H v I)·(~H v J)                  2, Dist.
     4. ~H v I                             3, Simp.
     5. H ⊃ I                              4, Impl.
 6.  1. N ⊃ O             /∴ (N·P) ⊃ O
     2. (N ⊃ O) v ~P                       1, Add.
     3. ~P v (N ⊃ O)                       2, Com.
     4. P ⊃ (N ⊃ O)                        3, Impl.
     5. (P·N) ⊃ O                          4, Exp.
     6. (N·P) ⊃ O                          5, Com.
 7.  1. (Q v R) ⊃ S       /∴ Q ⊃ S
     2. ~(Q v R) v S                       1, Impl.
     3. S v ~(Q v R)                       2, Com.
     4. S v (~Q ·~R)                       3, De M.
     5. (S v ~Q)·(S v ~R)                  4, Dist.
     6. S v ~Q                             5, Simp.
     7. ~Q v S                             6, Com.

     8. Q ⊃ S                              7, Impl.
 8.  1. T ⊃ U
     2. T ⊃ V             /∴ T ⊃ (U·V)
     3. (T ⊃ U)·(T ⊃ V)                    1, 2, Conj.
     4. (~T v U)·(~T v V)                  3, Impl.
     5. ~T v (U·V)                         4, Dist.
     6. T ⊃ (U·V)                          5, Impl.
 9.  1. W ⊃ X
     2. Y ⊃ X             /∴ (W v Y) ⊃ X
     3. (W ⊃ X)·(Y ⊃ X)                    1, 2, Conj.
     4. (~W v X)·(~Y v X)                  3, Impl.
     5. (X v~W)·(X v ~Y)                   4, Com.
     6. X v (~W·~Y)                        5, Dist.
     7. (~W·~Y) v X                        6, Com.
     8. ~(W v Y) v X                       7, De M.
     9. (W v Y) ⊃ X                        8, Impl.
10.  1. Z ⊃ A
     2. Z v A             /∴ A
     3. A v Z                              2, Com.
     4. ~~A v Z                            3, D.N.
     5. ~A ⊃ Z                             4, Impl.
     6. ~A ⊃ A                             5, 1, H.S.
     7. ~~A v A                            6, Impl.
     8. A v A                              7, D.N.
     9. A                                  8, Taut.
IV. 2.  1. D ⊃ (E v F)
        2. ~E·~F          /∴ ~D
        3. ~(E v F)                        2, De M.
```

```
      4.  ~D                                1, 3, M.T.
  3.  1.  (G  ⊃ ~H) ⊃  I
      2.  ~G v~H               /∴ I
      3.  G  ⊃ ~H                            2, Impl.
      4.  I                                  1, 3, M.P.
  4.  1.  (J v K) ⊃ ~L
      2.  L                     /∴  ~J
      3.  ~~L                                2, D.N.
      4.  ~(J v K)                           1, 3, M.T.
      5.  ~J·~K                              4, De M.
      6.  ~J                                 5, Simp.
  6.  1.  R v (S·~T)
      2.  (R v S) ⊃ (U v ~T)     /∴. T ⊃ U
      3.  (R v S)·(R v ~T)                   1, Dist.
      4.  R v S                              3, Simp.
      5.  U v ~T                             2, 4, M.P.
      6.  ~T v U                             5, Com.
      7.  T ⊃ U                              6, Impl.
  7.  1.  (~V ⊃ W)·(X ⊃ W)
      2.  ~(~X·V)                /∴  W
      3.  ~~X v ~V                           2, De M.
      4.  X v~V                              3, D.N.
      5.  ~V v X                             4, Com.
      6.  W v W                              1, 5, C.D.
      7.  W                                  6, Taut.
  8.  1.  [(Y·Z) ⊃ A]·[(Y·B) ⊃ C]
      2.  (B v Z)·Y              /∴. A v C
      3.  Y·(B v Z)                          2, Com.
      4.  Y·(Z v B)                          3, Com.
      5.  (Y·Z) v (Y·B)                      4, Dist.
      6.  A v C                              1, 5, C.D.
  9.  1.  ~D ⊃ (~E ⊃ ~F)
      2.  ~(F·~D) ⊃ ~G  /∴. G ⊃ E
      3.  ~D ⊃ (F ⊃ E)                       1, Trans.
      4.  (~D·F) ⊃ E                         3, Exp.
      5.  (F·~D) ⊃ E                         4, Com.
      6.  G ⊃ (F·~D)                         2, Trans.
      7.  G ⊃ E                              6, 5, H.S.
 11.  1.  M ⊃ N
      2.  M ⊃ (N ⊃ O) /∴. M ⊃ O
      3.  M ⊃ (M·N)                          1, Abs.
      4.  (M·N) ⊃ O                          2, Exp.
      5.  M ⊃ O                              3, 4, H.S.
 12.  1.  (P ⊃ Q)·(P v R)
      2.  (R ⊃ S)·(R v P) /∴. Q v S
      3.  P ⊃ Q                              1, Simp.
      4.  R ⊃ S                              2, Simp.
      5.  (P ⊃ Q)·(R ⊃ S)                    3, 4, Conj.
      6.  (P v R)·(P ⊃ Q)                    1, Com.
      7.  P v R                              6, Simp.
      8.  Q v S                              5, 7, C.D.
```

```
13.  1.  T  ⊃  (U·V)
     2.  (U v V)  ⊃  W       /∴  T  ⊃  W
     3.  ~T v (U·V)                       1, Impl.
     4.  (~T v U)·(~T v V)                3, Dist.
     5.  ~T v U                           4, Simp.
     6.  (~T v U) v V                     5, Add.
     7.  ~T v (U v V)                     6, Assoc.
     8.  T  ⊃  (U v V)                    7, Impl.
     9.  T  ⊃  W                          8, 2, H.S.
14.  1.  (X v Y)  ⊃  (X·Y)
     2.  ~(X v Y)            /∴  ~(X·Y)
     3.  ~X·~Y                            2, De M.
     4.  ~X                               3, Simp.
     5.  ~X v ~Y                          4, Add.
     6.  ~(X·Y)                           5, De M.
16.  1.  ~B v [(C ⊃ D)·(E ⊃ D)]
     2.  B·(C v E)           /∴  D
     3.  B                                2, Simp.
     4.  ~~B                              3, D.N.
     5.  (C ⊃ D)·(E ⊃ D)                  1, 4, D.S.
     6.  (C v E)·B                        2, Com.
     7.  C v E                            6, Simp.
     8.  D v D                            5, 7, C.D.
     9.  D                                8, Taut.
17.  1.  ~F v~[~(G·H)·(G v H)]
     2.  (G ⊃ H) ⊃ [(H ⊃ G) ⊃ I]  /∴  F ⊃ (F·I)
     3.  F  ⊃ ~[~(G·H)·(G vH)]            1, Impl.
     4.  F  ⊃ [~~(G·H) v ~(G v H)]        3, De M.
     5.  F  ⊃ [(G·H) v ~(G v H)]          4, D.N.
     6.  F  ⊃ [(G·H) v (~G·~H)]           5, De M.
     7.  F  ⊃ (G ≡ H)                     6, Equiv.
     8.  [(G ⊃ H)·(H ⊃ G)] ⊃ I           2, Exp.
     9.  (G ≡H) ⊃ I                       8, Equiv.
    10.  F ⊃ I                            7, 9, H.S.
    11.  F  ⊃ (F·I)                       10, Abs
18.  1.  J v (~J·K)
     2.  J ⊃ L              /∴  (L·J) ≡ J
     3.  J ⊃ (J·L)                        2, Abs.
     4.  J ⊃ (L·J)                        3, Com.
     5.  (J v~J)·(J v K)                  1, Dist.
     6.  J v ~J                           5, Simp.
     7.  ~J v J                           6, Com.
     8.  (~J v J) v ~L                    7, Add.
     9.  ~L v (~J v J)                    8, Com.
    10.  (~L v ~J) v J                    9, Assoc.
    11.  ~(L·J) v J                       10, De M
    12.  (L·J) ⊃ J                        11, Impl.
    13.  [(L·J) ⊃ J]·[J ⊃ (L·J)]          12, 4, Conj.
    14.  (L·J) ≡ J                        13, Equiv.
19.  1.  (M ⊃ N)·(O ⊃ P)
     2.  ~N v ~P
```

105

```
      3. ~(M·O)  ⊃  Q          /∴  Q
      4. (~N  ⊃  ~M)·(O  ⊃  P)                    1, Trans.
      5. (~N  ⊃  ~M)·(~P  ⊃  ~O)                  4, Trans.
      6. ~M v ~O                                  5, 2, C.D.
      7. ~(M·O)                                   6, De M.
      8. Q                                        3, 7, M.P.
20.   1. (R v S)  ⊃  (T·U)
      2. ~R  ⊃  (V  ⊃  ~V)
      3. ~T                      /∴ ~V
      4. ~T v ~U                                  3, Add.
      5. ~(T·U)                                   4, De M.
      6. ~(R v S)                                 1, 5, M.T.
      7. ~R·~S                                    6, De M.
      8. ~R                                       7, Simp.
      9. V  ⊃  ~V                                 2, 8, M.P.
     10. ~V v ~V                                  9, Impl.
     11. ~V                                      10, Taut.
V. 2. 1. C v V
      2. ~V                       /∴  C
      3. V v C                                    1, Com.
      4. C                                        3, 2, D.S.
   3. 1. (~A  ⊃  D)·(A  ⊃  I)
      2. A v ~A                   /∴  D v I
      3. ~A v A                                   2, Com.
      4. D v I                                    1, 3, C.D.
   4. 1. ~(F v~A)                 /∴  A
      2. ~F·~~A                                   1, De M.
      3. ~~A·~F                                   2, Com.
      4. ~~A                                      3, Simp.
      5. A                                        4, D.N.
   6. 1. F  ⊃  R
      2. R  ⊃  ~E
      3. F                        /∴  ~ E
      4. R                                        1, 3, M.P.
      5. ~E                                       2, 4, M.P.
   7. 1. M  ⊃  ~ R
      2. R v V
      3. M                        /∴  V
      4. ~R                                       1, 3, M.P.
      5. V                                        2, 4, D.S.
   8. 1. U  ⊃  C
      2. L v U
      3. ~L                       /∴  C
      4. U                                        2, 3, D.S.
      5. C                                        1, 4, M.P.
   9. 1. C  ⊃  M
      2. M  ⊃  P
      3. P  ⊃  I                  /∴  C  ⊃  I
      4. C  ⊃  P                                  1, 2, H.S.
      5. C  ⊃  I                                  4, 3, H.S.
```

```
11.  1. G ⊃ F
     2. F ⊃ ~P
     3. P                    /∴ ~ G
     4. G ⊃ ~P               1, 2, H.S.
     5. ~~P ⊃ ~G             4, Trans.
     6. P ⊃ ~G               5, D.N.
     7. ~G                   6, 3, M.P.
12.  1. F ⊃ W      /∴ (F·S) ⊃ W
     2. (F ⊃ W) v ~S         1, Add.
     3. ~S v (F ⊃ W)         2, Com.
     4. S ⊃ (F ⊃ W)          3, Impl.
     5. (S·F) ⊃ W            4, Exp.
     6. (F·S) ⊃ W            5, Com.
13.  1. (C ⊃ H)·(A ⊃ L)
     2. (H·L) ⊃ O
     3. ~O                   /∴ ~C v ~A
     4. ~(H·L)               2, 3, M.T.
     5. ~H v ~L              4, De M.
     6. (~H ⊃ ~C)·(~L ⊃ ~A)  1, Trans.
     7. ~C v ~A              6, 5, C.D.
14.  1. I ⊃ (M ⊃ C)
     2. ~C·I                 /∴ ~ M
     3. ~C                   2, Simp.
     4. I·~C                 2, Com.
     5. I                    4, Simp.
     6. M ⊃ C                1, 5, M.P.
     7. ~M                   6, 3, M.T.
16.  1. (T v C) ⊃ (V·P)
     2. P ⊃ O
     3. ~O                   /∴ ~ T
     4. ~P                   2, 3, M.T.
     5. ~P v ~V              4, Add.
     6. ~V v ~P              5, Com.
     7. ~(V·P)               6, De M.
     8. ~(T v C)             1, 7, M.T.
     9. ~T·~C                8, De M.
    10. ~T                   9, Simp.
17.  1. (D ⊃ F)·(P ⊃ N)
     2. D v P
     3. (D ⊃ ~N)·(P ⊃ ~F)   /∴ F ≡ ~N
     4. F v N                1, 2, C.D.
     5. ~N v ~F              3, 2, C.D.
     6. N v F                4, Com.
     7. ~~N v F              6, D.N.
     8. ~N ⊃ F               7, Impl.
     9. ~F v ~N              5, Com.
    10. F ⊃ ~N               9, Impl.
    11. (F ⊃ ~N)·(~N ⊃ F)    10, 8, Conj.
    12. F ≡ ~N               11, Equiv.
18.  1. W·(A·M)
     2. (A·W) ⊃ [N v (R v H)]
     3. ~N·(~P·~H)           /∴ R
```
107

	4.	(W·A)·M	1, Assoc.
	5.	W·A	4, Simp.
	6.	A·W	5, Com.
	7.	N v (R v H)	2, 6, M.P.
	8.	~N	3, Simp.
	9.	R v H	7, 8, D.S.
	10.	H v R	9, Com.
	11.	(~N·~P)·~H	3, Assoc.
	12.	~H·(~N·~P)	11, Com.
	13.	~H	12, Simp.
	14.	R	10, 13, D.S.
19.	1.	D v (I·S)	
	2.	(D ⊃ L)·(L ⊃ S) /∴ S	
	3.	(L ⊃ S)·(D ⊃ L)	2, Com.
	4.	D ⊃ L	2, Simp.
	5.	L ⊃ S	3, Simp.
	6.	D ⊃ S	4, 5, H.S.
	7.	D v (S·I)	1, Com.
	8.	(D v S)·(D v I)	7, Dist.
	9.	D v S	8, Simp.
	10.	S v D	9, Com.
	11.	~~S v D	10, D.N.
	12.	~S ⊃ D	11, Impl.
	13.	~S ⊃ S	12, 6, H.S.
	14.	~~S v S	13, Impl.
	15.	S v S	14, D.N.
	16.	S	15, Taut.
21.	1.	(H ⊃ P)·(S ⊃ W) /∴ (H v S) ⊃ (P v W)	
	2.	(~H v P)·(~S v W)	1, Impl.
	3.	~H v P	2, Simp.
	4.	(~H v P) v W	3, Add.
	5.	~H v (P v W)	4, Assoc.
	6.	(~S v W)·(~H v P)	2, Com.
	7.	~S v W	6, Simp.
	8.	(~S v W) v P	7, Add.
	9.	~S v (W v P)	8, Assoc.
	10.	~S v (P v W)	9, Com.
	11.	[~H v (P v W)]·[~S v (P v W)]	5, 10, Conj.
	12.	[(P v W) v ~H]·[(P v W) v ~S]	11, Com.
	13.	(P v W) v (~H·~S)	12, Dist.
	14.	(~H·~S) v (P v W)	13, Com.
	15.	~(H v S) v (P v W)	14, De M.
	16.	(H v S) ⊃ (P v W)	15, Impl.
22.	1.	(H ⊃ P)·(S ⊃ W) /∴ (H·S) ⊃ (P·W)	
	2.	(~H v P)·(~S v W)	1, Impl.
	3.	~H v P	2, Simp.
	4.	(~H v P) v ~S	3, Add.
	5.	~H v (P v ~S)	4, Assoc.
	6.	~H v (~S v P)	5, Com.
	7.	(~H v ~S) v P	6, Assoc.

```
        8.  (~S v W)·(~H v P)                    2, Com.
        9.  ~S v W                               8, Simp.
       10.  (~S v W) v ~H                        9, Add.
       11.  ~H v (~S v W)                       10, Com.
       12.  (~H v ~S) v W                       11, Assoc.
       13.  [(~H v ~S) v P]·[(~H v~S) v W]       7, 12, Conj.
       14.  (~H v ~S) v (P·W)                   13, Dist.
       15.  ~(H·S) v (P·W)                      14, De M.
       16.  (H·S) ⊃ (P·W)                       15, Impl.
23.     1.  F ⊃ ~A
        2.  F ⊃ (~A ⊃ ~P)

        3.  ~A ⊃ (~P ⊃ ~ C)      /∴ F ⊃ ~C
        4.  F ⊃ (F · ~A)                         1, Abs.
        5.  (F·~A) ⊃ ~P                          2, Exp.
        6.  F ⊃ ~P                               4, 5, H.S.
        7.  F ⊃ (~P ⊃ ~C)                        1, 3, H.S.
        8.  F ⊃ (F · ~P)                         6, Abs.
        9.  (F·~P) ⊃ ~C                          7, Exp.
       10.  F ⊃ ~C                               8, 9, H.S.
24.     1.  G                      /∴ H v ~H
        2.  G v ~H                               1, Add.
        3.  ~H v G                               2, Com.
        4.  H ⊃ G                                3, Impl.
        5.  H ⊃ (H·G)                            4, Abs.
        6.  ~H v (H·G)                           5, Impl.
        7.  (~H v H)·(~H v G)                    6, Dist.
        8.  ~H v H                               7, Simp.
        9.  H v ~H                               8, Com.
25.     1.  (H v ~H) ⊃ G    /∴ G
        2.  [(H v ~H) ⊃ G] v ~H                  1, Add.
        3.  ~H v [(H v ~H) ⊃ G]                  2, Com.
        4.  H ⊃ [(H v ~H) ⊃ G]                   3, Impl.
        5.  H ⊃ {H·[(H v ~H) ⊃ G]}              4, Abs.
        6.  ~H v {H·[(H v ~H) ⊃ G]}             5, Impl.
        7.  (~H v H)·{~H v [(H v ~H) ⊃ G]}      6, Dist.
        8.  ~H v H                               7, Simp.
        9.  H v ~H                               8, Com.
       10.  G                                    1, 9, M.P.
```

Exercises on page 332

```
    2.   E F G H              3.   I J K L        4.   M N O P Q R
         t f f f                   t f f f             t f t f f f
      or f t f f

    6.   A B C                7.   D E F G H I J   8.   K L M N O P Q R
         f f f                     t t t f t f f        t t t t f f f f
                               or  t t t f f f f
                               or  t t f f t f f
                               or  t t f f f f f

    9.   S T U V W X Y Z      10.  A B C D E F G H I J
         t t t f t f f t           t t f t f t f t f t
      or t t t f f f f t        or f t t t f t f t f t
                               or f t f t f t f t f t
```

Exercises on pages 336-339

I. 2. E F G H   3. I J K L
        t t f f   t t f f
     or f f t t   or t f t f

    4. 1. M ⊃ (N·O)
        2. (N v O) ⊃ P   /∴. M ⊃ P
        3. ~M v (N·O)   1, Impl.
        4. (~M v N)·(~M v O)   3, Dist.
        5. ~M v N   4, Simp.
        6. (~M v N) v O   5, Add.
        7. ~M v (N v O)   6, Assoc.
        8. M ⊃ (N v O)   7, Impl.
        9. M ⊃ P   8, 2, H.S.

    6. 1. [(D v E)·F] ⊃ G
        2. (F ⊃ G) ⊃ (H ⊃ I)
        3. H   /∴. D ⊃ I
        4. (D v E) ⊃ (F ⊃ G)   1, Exp.
        5. ~(D v E) v (F ⊃ G)   4, Impl.
        6. (F ⊃ G) v ~(D v E)   5, Com.
        7. (F ⊃ G) v (~D·~E)   6, De M.
        8. [(F ⊃ G) v ~D]·[(F ⊃ G) v ~E]   7, Dist.
        9. (F ⊃ G) v ~D   8, Simp.
       10. D v (F ⊃ G)   9, Com.
       11. D ⊃ (F ⊃ G)   10, Impl.
       12. D ⊃ (H ⊃ I)   11, 2, H.S.
       13. (D·H) ⊃ I   12, Exp.
       14. (H·D) ⊃ I   13, Com.
       15. H ⊃ (D ⊃ I)   14, Exp.
       16. D ⊃ I   15, 3, M.P.

    7. 1. (J·K) ⊃ (L ⊃ M)
        2. N ⊃ ~M
        3. ~(K ⊃ ~N)
        4. ~(J ⊃ ~L)   /∴. ~J
        5. ~(~K v ~N)   3, Impl.
        6. ~~K·~~N   5, De M.
        7. K·~~N   6, D.N.
        8. K·N   7, D.N.
        9. K   8, Simp.
       10. N·K   8, Com.
       11. N   10, Simp.
       12. ~(~J v ~L)   4, Impl.
       13. ~~J·~~L   12, De M.
       14. J·~~L   13, D.N.
       15. J   14, Simp.
       16. ~~L·J   14, Com.
       17. ~~L   16, Simp.
       18. J·K   15, 9, Conj.
       19. L ⊃ M   1, 18, M.P.
       20. ~M   2, 11, M.P.
       21. ~L   19, 20, M.T.
       22. ~L v ~J   21, Add.

110

```
       23. ~J                              22, 17, D.S.
  8.   O  P  Q  R  S
       t  t  f  f  t
  9.   1.  T  ⊃  (U·V)
       2.  U  ⊃  (W·X)
       3.  (T  ⊃  W)  ⊃  (Y ≡ Z)
       4.  (T  ⊃  U)  ⊃  ~Y
       5.  ~Y  ⊃  (~Z  ⊃  X)        /∴  X
       6.  ~T  v  (U·V)                     1, Impl.
       7.  (~T  v  U)·(~T  v  V)            6, Dist.
       8.  ~T  v  U                         7, Simp.
       9.  T  ⊃  U                          8, Impl.
      10.  ~Y                               4, 9, M.P.
      11.  ~Z  ⊃  X                         5, 10, M.P.
      12.  ~U  v  (W·X)                     2, Impl.
      13.  (~U  v  W)·(~U  v  X)            12, Dist.
      14.  ~U  v  W                         13, Simp.
      15.  U  ⊃  W                          14, Impl.
      16.  T  ⊃  W                          9, 15, H.S.
      17.  Y  ≡  Z                          3, 16, M.P.
      18.  (Y  ⊃  Z)·(Z  ⊃  Y)             17, Equiv.
      19.  (Z  ⊃  Y)·(Y  ⊃  Z)             18, Com.
      20.  Z  ⊃  Y                          19, Simp.
      21.  ~Z                               20, 10, M.T.
      22.  X                                11, 21, M.P.
 10.    A  B  C  D  E  F  G
        f  f  t  t  f  t  t
    or  f  f  t  f  f  t  t
    or  f  f  f  t  f  t  t
    or  f  f  f  f  f  t  t
II. 2.  1.  (O·T)  ⊃  (S  ⊃  M)
        2.  R  ⊃  ~M
        3.  T·R
        4.  O·S                      /∴  V
        5.  O                                4, Simp.
        6.  T                                3, Simp.
        7.  O·T                              5, 6, Conj.
        8.  S  ⊃  M                          1, 7, M.P.
        9.  S·O                              4, Com.
       10.  S                                9, Simp.
       11.  M                                8, 10, M.P.
       12.  R·T                              3, Com.
       13.  R                                12, Simp.
       14.  ~M                               2, 13, M.P.
       15.  M  v  V                          11, Add.
       16.  V                                15, 14, D.S.
    3.  1.  [(W·~A)  ⊃  I]·[(A·~W)  ⊃  M]
        2.  E  ⊃  (~W  v  ~A)
        3.  E
        4.  G  ⊃  (~I·~M)       /∴  ~G
```
proved invalid by the following assignment of truth

values:

$$\underline{\text{W A I M E G}}$$
$$\text{f f f f t t}$$

4. 1. (N v F) ⊃ (C·D)
    2. D ⊃ V
    3. V ⊃ I
    4. I ⊃ A
    5. A ⊃ ~C   /∴ ~F
    6. D ⊃ I   2, 3, H.S.
    7. D ⊃ A   6, 4, H.S.
    8. D ⊃ ~C   7, 5, H.S.
    9. ~D v ~C   8, Impl.
    10. ~C v ~D   9, Com.
    11. ~(C·D)   10, De M.
    12. ~(N v F)   1, 11, M.T.
    13. ~N·~F   12, De M.
    14. ~F·~N   13, Com.
    15. ~F   14, Simp.

6. 1. N ⊃ ~(M·G)
    2. [(P v D) ⊃ ~W]·[~W ⊃ ~(K v S)]
    3. ~G·(D·K)   /∴ ~N
    4. (D·K)·~G   3, Com.
    5. D·K   4, Simp.
    6. D   5, Simp.
    7. D v P   6, Add.
    8. P v D   7, Com.
    9. (P v D) ⊃ ~W   2, Simp.
    10. ~W   9, 8, M.P.
    11. [~W ⊃ ~(K v S)]·[(P v D) ⊃ ~W]   2, Com.
    12. ~W ⊃ ~(K v S)   11, Simp.
    13. ~(K v S)   12, 10, M.P.
    14. ~K·~S   13, De M.
    15. ~K   14, Simp.
    16. K·D   5, Com.
    17. K   16, Simp.
    18. K v ~N   17, Add.
    19. ~N   18, 15, D.S.

7. 1. (P ⊃ S)·(S ⊃ Q)
    2. (Q ⊃ R)·(R ⊃ H)
    3. ~H
    4. [(~S·~H) ⊃ D]·(D ⊃ P)   /∴ Q
    5. (S ⊃ Q)·(P ⊃ S)   1, Com.
    6. (R ⊃ H)·(Q ⊃ R)   2, Com.
    7. (D ⊃ P)·[(~S·~H) ⊃ D]   4, Com.
    8. S ⊃ Q   5, Simp.
    9. Q ⊃ R   2, Simp.
    10. S ⊃ R   8, 9, H.S.
    11. R ⊃ H   6, Simp.
    12. S ⊃ H   10, 11, H.S.
    13. ~S   12, 3, M.T.

112

```
     14.  ~S·~H                                    13, 3, Conj.
     15.  (~S·~H) ⊃ D                              4, Simp.
     16.  D                                         15, 14, M.P.
     17.  D ⊃ P                                     7, Simp.
     18.  P ⊃ S                                     1, Simp.
     19.  D ⊃ S                                     17, 18, H.S.
     20.  D ⊃ Q                                     19, 8, H.S.
     21.  Q                                         20, 16, M.P.
 8.   1.  (B ⊃ W)·(G ⊃ ~S)
      2.  (~B·~G) ⊃ (C·P)
      3.  ~W
      4.  P                        /∴  C  ⊃ ~G
          proved invalid by the following assignment of
          truth values:
                        B W G S C P
                        ─────────────
                        f f t f t t
 9.   1.  (F ⊃ L)·(~L v F)
      2.  (F·L) ⊃ (D·P)
      3.  (~F · ~L) ⊃ I
      4.  (I ⊃ C)·(C ⊃ P)      / ∴P
      5.  (C ⊃ P)·(I ⊃ C)                          4, Com.
      6.  I ⊃ C                                     4, Simp.
      7.  C ⊃ P                                     5, Simp.
      8.  I ⊃ P                                     6, 7, H.S.
      9.  (~F ·~L) ⊃ P                              3, 8, H.S.
     10.  (F ⊃ L)·(L ⊃ F)                           1, Impl.
     11.  F ≡ L                                     10, Equiv.
     12.  (F·L) v (~F· ~L)                          11, Equiv.
     13.  [(F·L) ⊃ (D·P)]·[(~F · ~L) ⊃ P] 2, 9, Conj.
     14.  (D·P) v P                                 13, 12, C.D.
     15.  P v (D·P)                                 14, Com.
     16.  P v (P·D)                                 15, Com.
     17.  (P v P)·(P v D)                           16, Dist.
     18.  P v P                                     17, Simp.
     19.  P                                         18, Taut.
11.   1.  L ⊃ H
      2.  L ⊃ (H ⊃ F)
      3.  H ⊃ (F ⊃ D)     /∴ L ⊃ D
      4.  L ⊃ (L·H)                                 1, Abs.
      5.  (L·H) ⊃ F                                 2, Exp.
      6.  L ⊃ F                                     4, 5, H.S.
      7.  L ⊃ (F ⊃ D)                               1, 3, H.S.
      8.  L ⊃ (L·F)                                 6, Abs.
      9.  (L·F) ⊃ D                                 7, Exp.
     10.  L ⊃ D                                     8, 9, H.S.
12.   1.  (L ⊃ H)·(Q ⊃ S)  /∴ (L·Q) ⊃ (H·S)
      2.  L ⊃ H                                     1, Simp.
      3.  ~L v H                                    2, Impl.
      4.  (~L v H) v ~Q                             3, Add.
      5.  ~L v (H v~Q)                              4, Assoc.
      6.  ~L v (~Q v H)                             5, Com.
```

113

```
        7.  (~L v ~Q) v H                          6, Assoc.
        8.  (Q ⊃ S)·(L ⊃ H)                        1, Com.
        9.  Q ⊃ S                                   8, Simp.
       10.  ~Q v S                                  9, Impl.
       11.  (~Q v S) v ~L                          10, Add.
       12.  ~L v (~Q v S)                          11, Com.
       13.  (~L v ~Q) v S                          12, Assoc.
       14.  [(~L v ~Q) v H]·[(~L v ~Q) v S]    7, 13, Conj.
       15.  (~L v ~Q) v (H·S)                      14, Dist.
       16.  ~(L·Q) v (H·S)                         15, De M.
       17.  (L·Q) ⊃ (H·S)                          16, Impl.
13.     1.  (L ⊃ H)·(Q ⊃ S)    /∴ (L v Q) ⊃ (H v S)
        2.  L ⊃ H                                   1, Simp.
        3.  ~L v H                                  2, Impl.
        4.  (~L v H) v S                            3, Add.
        5.  ~L v (H v S)                            4, Assoc.
        6.  (H v S) v ~L                            5, Com.
        7.  (Q ⊃ S)·(L ⊃ H)                        1, Com.
        8.  Q ⊃ S                                   7, Simp.
        9.  ~Q v S                                  8, Impl.
       10.  (~Q v S) v H                            9, Add.
       11.  ~Q v (S v H)                           10, Assoc.
       12.  ~Q v (H v S)                           11, Com.
       13.  (H v S) v ~Q                           12, Com.
       14.  [(H v S) v ~L]·[(H v S) v ~Q]     6, 13, Conj.
       15.  (H v S) v (~L · ~Q)                    14, Dist.
       16.  (~L · ~Q) v (H v S)                    15, Com.
       17.  ~(L v Q) v (H v S)                     16, De M.
       18.  (L v Q) ⊃ (H v S)                      17, Impl.
14.     1.  J ⊃ (A v S)
        2.  K ⊃ (S v I)
        3.  ~S              /∴ (~A · ~I) ⊃ (~J · ~K)
        4.  ~J v (A v S)                            1, Impl.
        5.  (~J v A) v S                            4, Assoc.
        6.  S v (~J v A)                            5, Com.
        7.  ~J v A                                  6, 3, D.S.
        8.  (~J v A) v I                            7, Add.
        9.  ~J v (A v I)                            8, Assoc.
       10.  (A v I) v ~J                            9, Com.
       11.  ~K v (S v I)                            2, Impl.
       12.  (S v I) v ~K                           11, Com.
       13.  S v (I v ~K)                           12, Assoc.
       14.  I v ~K                                 13, 3, D.S.
       15.  (I v ~K) v A                           14, Add.
       16.  A v (I v ~K)                           15, Com.
       17.  (A v I) v ~K                           16, Assoc.
       18.  [(A v I) v ~J]·[(A v I) v ~K]    10, 17, Conj.
       19.  (A v I) v (~J · ~K)                    18, Dist.
       20.  ~~(A v I) v (~J · ~K)                  19, D.N.
       21.  ~(~A · ~I) v (~J·~K)                   20, De M.
```

```
        22. (~A·~I) ⊃ (~J · ~K)              21, Impl.
  15.  1. (J v A) ⊃ [(S v K) ⊃ (~I·Y)]
       2. (~I v ~M) ⊃ E              / ∴ J ⊃ (S ⊃ E)
       3. ~(J v A) v [(S v K) ⊃ (~I·Y)]       1, Impl.
       4. [(S v K) ⊃ (~I·Y)] v ~(J v A)       3, Com.
       5. [(S v K) ⊃ (~I·Y)] v (~J · ~A)      4, De M.
       6. {[(S v K) ⊃ (~I·Y)] v ~J}·
              {[(S v K) ⊃ (~I·Y)] v ~A}       5, Dist.
       7. [(S v K) ⊃ (~I·Y)] v ~J             6, Simp.
       8. [~(S v K) v (~I·Y)] v ~J            7, Impl.
       9. ~(S v K) v [(~I·Y) v ~J]            8, Assoc.
      10. [(~I·Y) v ~J] v ~(S v K)            9, Com.
      11. [(~I·Y) v ~J] v (~S · ~K)          10, De M.
      12. {[(~I·Y) v ~J] v ~S}·
              {[(~I·Y) v ~J] v ~K}           11, Dist.
      13. [(~I·Y) v ~J] v ~S                 12, Simp.
      14. (~I·Y) v (~J v ~S)                 13, Assoc.
      15. (~J v ~S) v (~I·Y)                 14, Com.
      16. [(~J v ~S) v ~I]·[(~J v ~S) v Y]   15, Dist.
      17. (~J v ~S) v ~I                     16, Simp.
      18. [(~J v ~S) v ~I] v ~M              17, Add.
      19. (~J v ~S) v (~I v ~M)              18, Assoc.
      20. ~(J·S) v (~I v ~M)                 19, De M.
      21. (J·S) ⊃ (~I v ~M)                  20, Impl.
      22. (J·S) ⊃ E                          21, 2, H.S.
      23. J ⊃ (S ⊃ E)                        22, Exp.
  16.  1. W              / ∴  R v ~R
       2. W v ~R                              1, Add.
       3. ~R v W                              2, Com.
       4. R ⊃ W                               3, Impl.
       5. R ⊃ (R·W)                           4, Abs.
       6. ~R v (R·W)                          5, Impl.
       7. (~R v R)·(~R v W)                   6, Dist.
       8. ~R v R                              7, Simp.
       9. R v ~R                              8, Com.
  17.  1. (R v ~R) ⊃ W          / ∴   W
       2. [(R v ~R) ⊃ W] v ~R                 1, Add.
       3. ~R v [(R v ~R) ⊃ W]                 2, Com.
       4. R ⊃ [(R v ~R) ⊃ W]                  3, Impl.
       5. R ⊃ {R·[(R v ~R) ⊃ W]}             4, Abs.
       6. ~R v {R · [(R v ~R) ⊃ W]}          5, Impl.
       7. (~R v R)·{~R v [(R v ~R) ⊃ W]}     6, Dist.
       8. ~R v R                              7, Simp.

       9. R v ~R                              8, Com.
      10. W                                   1, 9, M.P.
```

Exercises on pages 352-353

```
 I. 2. (x)(Sx  ⊃ ~Mx)        3. (∃x)(Rx·Px)
    4. (x)(Nx ⊃ Cx)          6. (x)(Ax ⊃ Dx)
    7. (x)(Bx ⊃ ~Cx)         8. (x)(Cx ⊃ Lx)
```

9. $(\exists x)(Sx \cdot Fx)$ 11. $(\exists x)(Cx \cdot Px)$
12. $(\exists x)(Cx \cdot \sim Px)$ 13. $(\exists x)(Gx \cdot \sim Ax)$
14. $(x)(Dx \supset Bx)$ 16. $(x)(Ex \supset Ux)$
17. $(\exists x)(Hx \cdot Px)$ 18. $(\exists x)(Ax \cdot \sim Hx)$
19. $(x)(Ax \supset \sim Hx)$ 20. $(x)(Ix \supset \sim Sx)$

II. 2. $(\exists x)(Cx \cdot Dx)$
  3. $(x)(\sim Ex \lor \sim Fx)$ or $(x)(Ex \supset \sim Fx)$
  4. $(x)(\sim Gx \lor Hx)$ or $(x)(Gx \supset Hx)$
  6. $(\exists x)(Kx \cdot Lx)$
  7. $(x)(Mx \lor Nx)$ or $(x)(\sim Mx \supset Nx)$
  8. $(x)(Ox \lor \sim Px)$ or $(x)(Px \supset Ox)$ or $(x)(\sim Ox \supset \sim Px)$
  9. $(x)(\sim Qx \lor Rx)$ or $(x)(Qx \supset Rx)$
  10. $(\exists x)(Sx \cdot \sim Tx)$
  11. $(\exists x)(\sim Ux \cdot \sim Vx)$
  12. $(x)(\sim Wx \lor \sim Xx)$ or $(x)(Wx \supset \sim Xx)$

Exercises on pages 360-361

I. 2. 1. $(x)(Dx \supset \sim Ex)$
  2. $(x)(Fx \supset Ex)$ $/\therefore (x)(Fx \supset \sim Dx)$
  3. $Fy \supset Ey$ 2, UI
  4. $Dy \supset \sim Ey$ 1, UI
  5. $\sim\sim Dy \supset \sim Ey$ 4, D.N.
  6. $Ey \supset \sim Dy$ 5, Trans.
  7. $Fy \supset \sim Dy$ 3, 6, H.S.
  8. $(x)(Fx \supset \sim Dx)$ 7, UG

  3. 1. $(x)(Fx \supset Hx)$
  2. $(x)(Ix \supset \sim Hx)$ $/\therefore (x)(Ix \supset \sim Gx)$
  3. $Iy \supset \sim Hy$ 2, UI
  4. $Gy \supset Hy$ 1, UI
  5. $\sim Hy \supset \sim Gy$ 4, Trans.
  6. $Iy \supset \sim Gy$ 3, 5, H.S.
  7. $(x)(Ix \supset \sim Gx)$ 6, UG

  4. 1. $(\exists x)(Jx \cdot Kx)$
  2. $(x)(Jx \supset Lx)$ $/\therefore (\exists x)(Lx \cdot Kx)$
  3. $Ja \cdot Ka$ 1, EI
  4. $Ja \supset La$ 2, UI
  5. Ja 3, Simp.
  6. La 4, 5, M.P.
  7. $Ka \cdot Ja$ 3, Com.
  8. Ka 7, Simp.
  9. $La \cdot Ka$ 6, 8. Conj.
  10. $(\exists x)(Lx \cdot Kx)$ 9, EG

  6. 1. $(\exists x)(Px \cdot \sim Qx)$
  2. $(x)(Px \supset Rx)$ $/\therefore (\exists x)(Rx \cdot \sim Qx)$
  3. $Pa \cdot \sim Qa$ 1, EI
  4. $Pa \supset Ra$ 2, UI
  5. Pa 3, Simp.
  6. Ra 4, 5, M.P.
  7. $\sim Qa \cdot Pa$ 3, Com.
  8. $\sim Qa$ 7, Simp.
  9. $Ra \cdot \sim Qa$ 6, 8, Conj.

116

```
      10. (∃x)(Rx· ~Qx)                        9, EG
 7.   1. (x)(Sx ⊃ ~Tx)
      2. (∃x)(Sx·Ux)          /∴ (∃x)(Ux .~Tx)
      3. Sa·Ua                                  2, EI
      4. Sa ⊃ ~Ta                               1, UI
      5. Sa                                     3, Simp.
      6. ~Ta                                    4, 5, M.P.
      7. Ua·Sa                                  3, Com.
      8. Ua                                     7, Simp.
      9. Ua·~Ta                                 8, 6, Conj.
     10. (∃x)(Ux·~Tx)                           9, EG
 8.   1. (x)(Vx ⊃ Wx)
      2. (x)(Wx ⊃ ~Xx)        /∴ (x)(Xx ⊃ ~Vx)
      3. Vy ⊃ Wy                                1, UI
      4. Wy ⊃ ~Xy                               2, UI
      5. Vy ⊃ ~Xy                               3, 4, H.S.
      6. ~~Xy ⊃ ~Vy                             5, Trans.
      7. Xy ⊃ ~Vy                               6, D.N.
      8. (x)(Xx ⊃ ~Vx)                          7, UG
 9.   1. (∃x)(Yx·Zx)
      2. (x)(Zx ⊃ Ax)         /∴ (∃x)(Ax·Yx)
      3. Ya·Za                                  1, EI
      4. Za ⊃ Aa                                2, UI
      5. Za.Ya                                  3, Com.
      6. Za                                     5, Simp.
      7. Aa                                     4, 6, M.P.
      8. Ya                                     3, Simp.
      9. Aa·Ya                                  7, 8, Conj.
     10. (∃x)(Ax·Yx)                            9, EG
10.   1. (x)(Bx ⊃ ~Cx)
      2. (∃x)(Cx·Dx)          /∴ (∃x)(Dx·~Bx)
      3. Ca·Da                                  2, EI
      4. Ba ⊃ ~Ca                               1, UI
      5. Ca                                     3, Simp.
      6. ~~Ca                                   5, D.N.
      7. ~Ba                                    4, 6, M.T.
      8. Da·Ca                                  3, Com.
      9. Da                                     8, Simp.
     10. Da·~Ba                                 9, 7, Conj.
     11. (∃x)(Dx·~Bx)                           10, EG
11.   1. (x)(Fx ⊃ Gx)
      2. (∃x)(Fx·~Gx)         /∴ (∃x)(Gx .~Fx)
      3. Fa·~Ga                                 2, EI
      4. Fa ⊃ Ga                                1, UI
      5. Fa                                     3, Simp.
      6. Ga                                     4, 5, M.P.
      7. ~Ga·Fa                                 3, Com.
      8. ~Ga                                    7, Simp.
      9. Ga v (∃x)(Gx·~Fx)                      6, Add.
     10. (∃x)(Gx·~Fx)                           9, 8, D.S.
```

II. 2. 1. (x)(Dx ⊃ Ex)
     2. (∃x)(Fx · ~Ex)   /∴ (∃x)(Fx · ~Dx)
     3. Fa·~Ea   2, EI
     4. Da ⊃ Ea   1, UI
     5. Fa   3, Simp.
     6. ~Ea·Fa   3, Com.
     7. ~Ea   6, Simp.
     8. ~Da   4, 7, M.T.
     9. Fa·~Da   5, 8, Conj.
    10. (∃x)(Fx·~Dx)   9, EG
  3. 1. (x)(Gx ⊃ ~Hx)
     2. (∃x)(Ix·Hx)   /∴ (∃x)(Ix· ~Gx)
     3. Ia·Ha   2, EI
     4. Ga ⊃ ~Ha   1, UI
     5. Ia   3, Simp.
     6. Ha·Ia   3, Com.
     7. Ha   6, Simp.
     8. ~~Ha   7, D.N.
     9. ~Ga   4, 8, M.T.
    10. Ia·~Ga   5, 9, Conj.
    11. (∃x)(Ix·~Gx)   10, EG
  4. 1. (x)(Jx ⊃ Kx)
     2. (x)(Kx ⊃ ~Lx) /∴ (x)(Jx ⊃ ~Lx)
     3. Jy ⊃ Ky   1, UI
     4. Ky ⊃ ~Ly   2, UI
     5. Jy ⊃ ~Ly   3, 4, H.S.
     6. (x)(Jx ⊃ ~Lx)   5, UG
  6. 1. (x)(Qx ⊃ Px)
     2. (∃x)(Qx·Rx)   /∴ (∃x)(Px·Rx)
     3. Qa·Ra   2, EI
     4. Qa ⊃ Pa   1, UI
     5. Qa   3, Simp.
     6. Pa   4, 5, M.P.
     7. Ra·Qa   3, Com.
     8. Ra   7, Simp.
     9. Pa·Ra   6, 8. Conj.
    10. (∃x)(Px·Rx)   9, EG
  7. 1. (x)(Sx ⊃ Tx)
     2. (x)(Tx ⊃ Ux) /∴ (x)(Sx ⊃ Ux)
     3. Sy ⊃ Ty   1, UI
     4. Ty ⊃ Uy   2, UI
     5. Sy ⊃ Uy   3, 4, H.S.
     6. (x)(Sx ⊃ Ux)   5, UG
  8. 1. (x)(Vx ⊃ Wx)
     2. (x)(Xx ⊃ ~Wx)   /∴ (x)(V x ⊃ ~Xx)
     3. Vy ⊃ Wy   1, UI
     4. Xy ⊃ ~Wy   2, UI
     5. ~~Wy ⊃ ~Xy   4, Trans.
     6. Wy ⊃ ~Xy   5, D.N.
     7. Vy ⊃ ~Xy   3, 6, H.S.

```
     8. (x)(Vx  ⊃ ~Xx)                              7, UG
 9.  1. (x)(Dx  ⊃ Bx)
     2. (x)(Bx  ⊃ Sx)        /∴  (x)(Dx  ⊃ Sx)
     3. Dy ⊃  By                                    1, UI
     4. By ⊃  Sy                                    2, UI
     5. Dy ⊃  Sy                                    3, 4, H.S.
     6. (x)(Dx  ⊃ Sx)                               5, UG
10.  1. (x)(Ax  ⊃ Rx)
     2. ~Rs                  /∴.~As
     3. As ⊃ Rs                                     1, UI
     4. ~As                                         3, 2, M.T.
```

Exercises on pages 365-366

```
 I.  2. logically equivalent in [a] to      Da ⊃  ~Ea
        and proved invalid by               Ea ⊃  Fa
        Da  Ea  Fa                          ∴.Fa ⊃ ~Da
        t   f   t
     3. logically equivalent in [a] to      Ga ⊃ Ha
        and proved invalid by               Ga ⊃ Ia
        Ga   Ha   Ia                        ∴.Ia ⊃  Ha
        f    f    t
     4. logically equivalent in [a, b] to (Ja·Ka) v (Jb·Kb)
        and proved invalid by             (Ka·La) v (Kb·Lb)
        Ja  Jb  Ka  Kb  La  Lb            ∴.(La·Ja) v (Lb·Jb)
        t   f   t   t   f   t
     or f   t   t   t   t   f
     6. logically equivalent in [a] to      Pa ⊃ ~ Qa
        and proved invalid by               Pa ⊃ ~ Ra
        Pa  Qa  Ra                          ∴.Ra ⊃ ~ Qa
        f   t   t
     7. logically equivalent in [a] to      Sa ⊃ ~Ta
        and proved invalid by               Ta ⊃ Ua
        Sa  Ta  Ua                          ∴.Ua· ~Sa
        t   f   t
        or any of several other truth value assignments.
     8. logically equivalent in [a, b] to   (Va·~Wa) v (Vb·~Wb)
        and proved invalid by               (Wa·~Xa) v (Wb·~Xb)
                                            ∴.(Xa·~Va) v (Xb·~Vb)

        Va  Vb  Wa  Wb  Xa  Xb
        t   t   f   t   t   f
        or any of several other truth value assignments.
     9. logically equivalent in [a] to      Ya·Za
        and proved invalid by               Aa·Za
        Ya  Za  Aa                          ∴.Aa· ~Ya
        t   t   t
    10. logically equivalent in [a, b], to
            (Ba·~Ca) v (Bb·~Cb)
            (Da ⊃  ~Ca)·(Db ⊃  ~Cb)
            ∴.(Da ⊃  Ba)·(Db ⊃  Bb)
        and proved invalid by
        Ba  Bb  Ca  Cb  Da  Db
        f   t   f   f   t   t
```

or any of several other truth value assignments.

II. 2. (x)(Dx ⊃ ~Ex)   Da ⊃ ~Ea

	Da	Ea	Fa
	f	t	t

    (∃x)(Fx·Ex)   Fa·Ea

    ∴(∃x)(Dx·~Fx)   ∴Da·~Fa

3. (x)(Gx ⊃ Hx)   Ga ⊃ Ha

	Ga	Ha	Ia
	f	t	t

    (∃x)(Ix·Hx)   Ia·Ha

    ∴(∃x)(Gx·Ix)   ∴Ga·Ia

4. (∃x)(Jx ·~Kx)   (Ja· ~Ka) v (Jb ·~Kb)

    (∃x)(Kx ·~Lx)   (Ka·~La) v (Kb·~Lb)

    ∴(∃x)(Jx ·~Lx)   ∴(Ja ·~La) v (Jb· ~Lb)

Ja	Jb	Ka	Kb	La	Lb
t	f	f	t	t	f

6. (∃x)(Px·Qx)   (Pa·Qa) v (Pb·Qb)

    (∃x)(Qx·~Rx)   (Qa ·~Ra) v (Qb ·~Rb)

    ∴(∃x)(Px·~Rx)   ∴(Pa ·~Ra) v (Pb·~Rb)

Pa	Pb	Qa	Qb	Ra	Rb
t	f	t	t	t	f

7. (∃x)(Px·Lx)   Pa·La

	Pa	La	Oa
	t	t	f

    (∃x)(Lx·~Ox)   La·~Oa

    ∴(∃x)(Ox·~Px)   ∴Oa·~Pa

8. (x)(Dx ⊃ Bx)   Da ⊃ Ba

	Da	Ba	Sa
	t	t	f

    (x)(Sx ⊃ Bx)   Sa ⊃ Ba

    ∴(x)(Dx ⊃ Sx)   ∴Da ⊃ Sa

9. (x)(Mx ⊃ Bx)   Ma ⊃ Ba

	Ma	Ba	Oa
	f	t	t

    (∃x)(Bx·Ox)   Ba·Oa

    ∴(∃x)(Mx·Ox)   ∴Ma·Oa

10. (x)(Mx ⊃ Sx)   Ma ⊃ Sa

	Ma	Sa	Wa
	t	t	f

    (x)(Wx ⊃ Mx)   Wa ⊃ Ma

    ∴(x)(Sx ⊃ Wx)   ∴Sa ⊃ Wa

Exercises on pages 369-373

I. 2. (∃x)[Fx·(Ex ⊃ Cx)]

3. (x)[Cx ⊃ (~Sx v Bx)]

4. (x){(Tx·Mx) ⊃ [(Dx·Hx) ⊃ Ax]}

6. (x){[Bx·(Wx ≡ Lx)] ⊃ ~Sx}

7. (∃x)[(Px·Wx)·~(Ex·Cx)]

8. (∃x)[(Tx·Cx)·~(Sx v Bx)]

9. (x)[(Px·Dx) ⊃ Cx]

10. (x){Ax ⊃ [(Bx ⊃ Wx)·(Px ⊃ Sx)]}

II. 2. logically equivalent in a, b to

    {(Ea·Fa)·[(Ea v Fa) ⊃ (Ga·Ha)]} v {(Eb·Fb)·[(Eb v Fb) ⊃ (Gb·Hb)]}

    ∴(Ea ⊃ Ha)·(Eb ⊃ Hb)

    proved invalid by

Ea	Eb	Fa	Fb	Ga	Gb	Ha	Hb
t	c	t	t	t	t	t	f

    or any of several other truth value assignments.

3. 1. (x){ [Ix ⊃ (Jx·~Kx)]·[Jx ⊃ (Ix ⊃ Kx)]}

   2. (∃x)[(Ix·Jx) ·~Lx]   /∴ (∃x)(Kx·Lx)

   3. (Ia·Ja)·~La   2, EI

   4. [Ia ⊃ (Ja·~Ka)]·[Ja ⊃ (Ia ⊃ Ka)]   1, UI

```
      5. Ia·Ja                              3, Simp.
      6. Ia  ⊃ (Ja·~Ka)                     4, Simp.
      7. Ia                                 5, Simp.
      8. Ja ·~Ka                            6, 7, M.P.
      9. {Ja ⊃ (Ia ⊃ Ka)]·[Ia ⊃ (Ja·~Ka)]  4, Com.
     10. Ja ⊃ (Ia ⊃ Ka)                     9, Simp.
     11. Ja                                 8, Simp.
     12. Ia ⊃ Ka                            10, 11, M.P.
     13. Ka                                 12, 7, M.P.
     14. Ka v (∃x)(Kx·Lx)                   13, Add.
     15. ~Ka.Ja                             8, Com.
     16. ~Ka                                15, Simp.
     17. (∃x)(Kx·Lx)                        14, 16, D.S.
```

4. logically equivalent in |a| to   (Ma·Na) ⊃ (Oa v Pa)
    and proved invalid by   (Oa·Pa) ⊃ (Qa v Ra)
    <u>Ma Na Oa Pa Qa Ra</u>   ∴(Ma v Oa) ⊃ Ra
     t f f f f f
    or any of several other truth value assignments.

6.
```
      1. (x)[Wx ⊃  (Xx ⊃ Yx)]
      2. (∃x)[Xx·(Zx · ~Ax)]
      3. (x)[(Wx ⊃ Yx) ⊃  (Bx ⊃  Ax)]  /∴ (∃x)(Zx · ~Bx)
      4. Xa·(Za · ~Aa)                   2, EI
      5. Wa ⊃ (Xa ⊃  Ya)                 1, UI
      6. (Wa ⊃ Ya) ⊃ (Ba ⊃ Aa)          3, UI
      7. (Wa·Xa) ⊃ Ya                    5, Exp.
      8. (Xa·Wa) ⊃ Ya                    7, Com.
      9. Xa ⊃ (Wa ⊃  Ya)                 8, Exp.
     10. Xa                              4, Simp.
     11. Wa ⊃  Ya                        9, 10, M.P.
     12. Ba ⊃  Aa                        6, 11, M.P.
     13. (Za·~Aa)·Xa                     4, Com.
     14. Za·~Aa                          13, Simp.
     15. Za                              14, Simp.
     16. ~Aa·Za                          14, Com.
     17. ~Aa                             16, Simp.
     18. ~Ba                             12, 17, M.T.
     19. Za·~Ba                          15, 18, Conj.
     20. (∃x)(Zx·~Bx)                    19, EG
```

7. logically equivalent in |a, b| to
    [Ca·~(Da ⊃ Ea)] v [Cb·~(Db ⊃ Eb)]
    [(Ca·Da) ⊃ Fa]·[(Cb·Db) ⊃ Fb]
    [Ea·~(Da ⊃ Ca)] v [Eb·~(Db ⊃ Cb)]
    (Ga ⊃ Ca)·(Gb ⊃ Cb)
    ∴(Ga·~Fa) v (Gb·~Fb)
    and proved invalid by
    <u>Ca Cb Da Db Ea Eb Fa Fb Ga Gb</u>
     t f t t f t t t t f
    or any of several other truth value assignments.

8.
```
      1. (x)(Hx ⊃  Ix)
      2. (x)[(Hx·Ix) ⊃  Jx]
```

```
      3. (x)[~Kx ⊃ (Hx v Ix)]
      4. (x)[(Jx v ~Jx) ⊃ (Ix ⊃  Hx)]   /∴ (x)(Jx v Kx)
      5. (Hy·Iy) ⊃ Jy                    2, UI
      6. ~Jy  ⊃ ~(Hy·Iy)                 5, Trans.
      7. ~Jy  ⊃ [~Jy·~(Hy·Iy)]           6, Abs.
      8. ~~Jy v [~Jy ·~(Hy·Iy)]          7, Impl.
      9. (~~Jy v ~Jy)·[~~Jy v ~(Hy·Iy)]  8, Dist.
     10. ~~Jy v ~Jy                      9, Simp.
     11. Jy v ~Jy                        10, D.N.
     12. (Jy v ~Jy) ⊃ (Iy ⊃  Hy)         4, UI
     13. Iy ⊃  Hy                        12, 11, M.P.
     14. Hy ⊃  Iy                        1, UI
     15. (Hy ⊃  Iy)·(Iy ⊃  Hy)           14, 13, Conj.
     16. Hy ≡ Iy                         15, Equiv.
     17. (Hy·Iy) v (~Hy·~Iy)             16, Equiv.
     18. ~Ky ⊃ (Hy v Iy)                 3, UI
     19. ~(Hy v Iy) ⊃  ~~Ky              18, Trans.
     20. ~(Hy v Iy) ⊃  Ky                19, D.N.
     21. (~Hy ·~Iy) ⊃  Ky                20, De M.
     22. [(Hy·Iy)  ⊃ Jy]·[(~Hy· ~Iy) ⊃  Ky]   5, 21, Conj.
     23. Jy v Ky                         22, 17, C.D.
     24. (x)(Jx v Kx)                    23, UG
  9.  1. (x){(Lx v Mx)  ⊃ {[(Nx·Ox) v Px]  ⊃ Qx}}
      2. (∃x)(Mx ·~Lx)
      3. (x){[(Ox ⊃ Qx)· ~Rx] ⊃ Mx}
      4. ( x)(Lx · ~Mx)          /∴ (∃x)(Nx ⊃  Rx)
      5. La·~Ma                           4, EI
      6. La                               5, Simp.
      7. La v Ma                          6, Add.
      8. (La v Ma)  ⊃ {[(Na·Oa) v Pa]  ⊃ Qa }   1, UI
      9. [(Na·Oa) v Pa] ⊃  Qa             8, 7, M.P.
     10. ~[(Na·Oa) v Pa] v Qa             9, Impl.
     11. Qa v ~[(Na·Oa) v Pa]             10, Com.
     12. Qa v [~(Na·Oa)· ~Pa]             11, De M.
     13. [Qa v ~(Na·Oa)]·(Qa v ~Pa)       12, Dist.
     14. Qa v ~(Na·Oa)                    13, Simp.
     15. ~(Na·Oa) v Qa                    14, Com.
     16. (Na·Oa) ⊃  Qa                    15, Impl.
     17. Na  ⊃ (Oa ⊃  Qa)                 16, Exp.
     18. [(Oa  ⊃ Qa)· ~Ra] ⊃ Ma           3, UI
     19. ~Ma·La                           5, Com.
     20. ~Ma                              19, Simp.
     21. ~[(Oa ⊃ Qa) ·~Ra]                18, 20, M.T.
     22. ~(Oa ⊃  Qa) v ~~Ra               21, De M.
     23. ~(Oa ⊃ Qa) v Ra                  22, D.N.
     24. (Oa ⊃ Qa) ⊃ Ra                   23, Impl.
     25. Na ⊃ Ra                          17, 24, H.S.
     26. (∃x)(Nx ⊃ Rx)                    25, EG
 10. logically equivalent in a, b  to
```

[(Sa v Ta) ⊃ ~(Ua v Va)].[(Sb v Tb) ⊃ ~(Ub v Vb)]
(Sa · ~Wa) v (Sb· ~Wb)
(Ta·~Xa) v (Tb·~Xb)
(~Wa ⊃ Xa)·(~Wb ⊃ Xb)
∴(Ua·~Va) v (Ub · ~Vb)
and proved invalid by

Sa	Sb	Ta	Tb	Ua	Ub	Va	Vb	Wa	Wb	Xa	Xb
t	t	t	t	f	f	f	f	f	t	t	f

or any of several other truth value assignments.

III. 2. 1. (x)[Tx ⊃ (Ex v Ux)]
          2. (∃x)(Tx · ~Ux)   /∴ (∃x)(Ex·Tx)
          3. Ta·~Ua   2, EI
          4. Ta ⊃ (Ea v Ua)   1, UI
          5. Ta   3, Simp.
          6. Ea v Ua   4, 5, M.P.
          7. ~Ua·Ta   3, Com.
          8. ~Ua   7, Simp.
          9. Ua v Ea   6, Com.
         10. Ea   9, 8, D.S.
         11. Ea·Ta   10, 5, Conj.
         12. (∃x)(Ex·Tx)   11, EG
      3. (x)[(Ax v Sx) ⊃ (Ox v Vx)] (Aa v Sa) ⊃ (Oa v Va)
         (∃x)(Sx·~Ox)   Sa·Oa
         ∴(∃x)(Ax·Vx)   ∴Aa·Va

Aa	Sa	Oa	Va
f	t	f	t

   4. 1. (x){[Ex·(Sx v Dx)] ⊃ ~Px} /∴ (x)[(Dx·Ex) ⊃ ~ Px]
       2. [Ey·(Sy v Dy)] ⊃ ~Py   1, UI
       3. ~[Ey·(Sy v Dy)] v ~Py   2, Impl.
       4. ~[Ey·(Dy v Sy)] v ~Py   3, Com.
       5. ~[(Ey·Dy) v (Ey·Sy)] v ~Py   4, Dist.
       6. ~Py v ~[(Ey·Dy) v (Ey·Sy)]   5, Com.
       7. ~Py v [~(Ey·Dy) · ~(Ey·Sy)]   6, De M.
       8. [~Py v ~(Ey·Dy)]·[~Py v~(Ey·Sy)]   7, Dist.
       9. ~Py v ~(Ey·Dy)   8, Simp.
      10. ~(Ey·Dy) v ~Py   9, Com.
      11. ~(Dy·Ey) v ~Py   10, Com.
      12. (Dy·Ey) ⊃ ~Py   11, Impl.
      13. (x)[(Dx·Ex) ⊃ ~Px]   12, UG
   6. 1. (x)(Gx ⊃ Ex)
       2. (x)(Wx ⊃ ~Sx)
       3.(∃x)(Wx·~Ex)   /∴ (∃x)[~(Gx v Sx)]
       4. Wa·~Ea   3, EI
       5. Wa ⊃ ~Sa   2, UI
       6. Wa   4, Simp.
       7. ~Sa   5, 6, M.P.
       8. ~Ea·Wa   4, Com.
       9. ~Ea   8, Simp.
      10. Ga ⊃ Ea   1, UI
      11. ~Ga   10, 9, M.T.
      12. ~Ga · ~Sa   11, 7, Conj.

123

```
       13. ~(Ga v Sa)                                      12, De M.
       14. (∃x)[~(Gx v Sx)]                                13, EG
  7.     (x)(Tx ⊃  Cx)              Ta ⊃  Ca
         (x)(Rx ⊃ ~Lx)             Ra  ⊃ ~La
         (∃x)[~(Tx v Lx)]          ~(Ta v La)
         ∴(∃x)(Rx·~Cx)             ∴Ra·~Ca
                              Ta Ca Ra La
                              f  t  t  f
  8.     (∃x)[Px·(Ax·~Ix)]       [Pa·(Aa·~Ia)] v [Pb·(Ab·~Ib)]
         (x)(Px  ⊃ Gx)           (Pa ⊃  Ga)·(Pb  ⊃ Gb)
         (∃x)(Px·~Ax)            (Pa·~Aa) v (Pb·~Ab)
         (x)(Sx ⊃ Ax)            (Sa  ⊃ Aa)·(Sb ⊃ Ab)
         ∴(∃x)(Sx·~Gx)           ∴(Sa· ~Ga) v (Sb·~Gb)
                        Pa Pb Aa Ab Ia Ib Ga Gb Sa Sb
                        t  t  t  f  f  t  t  t  t  f
  9. 1. (∃x)[Px·(Sx ·~Ix)]
     2. (x)(Px ⊃  Ax)
     3. (∃x)(Px·~Sx)
     4. (x)(Jx ⊃  Sx)              /∴  (∃x)(Ax ·~Jx)
     5. Pa·~Sa                                   3, EI
     6. Pa                                       5, Simp.
     7. Pa ⊃  Aa                                 2, UI
     8. Aa                                       7, 6, M.P.
     9. ~Sa·Pa                                   5, Com.
    10. ~Sa                                      9, Simp.
    11. Ja ⊃  Sa                                 4, UI
    12. ~Ja                                     11, 10, M.T.
    13. Aa·~Ja                                   8, 12, Conj.
    14. (∃x)(Ax·~Jx)                            13, EG
  10. 1. (x)[Bx  ⊃ (Ix ⊃ Wx)]
      2. (x)[Bx  ⊃ (Wx ⊃ Ix)]   /∴(x){Bx  ⊃
                            [(Ix v Wx) ⊃ (Ix·Wx)]}
      3. By ⊃ (Iy ⊃ Wy)                          1, UI
      4. By ⊃ (Wy ⊃ Iy)                          2, UI
      5. [By ⊃ (Iy ⊃ Wy)]·[By ⊃ (Wy ⊃ Iy)]      3, 4, Conj.
      6. [~By v (Iy ⊃ Wy)]·[~By v (Wy ⊃ Iy)]     5, Impl.
      7. ~By v [(Iy ⊃ Wy)·(Wy ⊃ Iy)]             6, Dist.
      8. ~By v (Iy ≡ Wy)                          7, Equiv.
      9. ~By v [(Iy·Wy) v (~Iy ·~Wy)]             8, Equiv.
     10. ~By v [(~Iy·~Wy) v (Iy·Wy)]             9, Com.
     11. ~By v [~(Iy v Wy) v (Iy·Wy)]           10, De M.
     12. By ⊃ [(Iy v Wy) ⊃ (Iy·Wy)]             11, Impl.
     13. (x){Bx ⊃ [(Ix v Wx) ⊃ (Ix·Wx)]}        12, UG
IV. 2. 1. (x)[(Dx v Lx) ⊃ Px]
       2. (x)[(Px v Ex) ⊃ Rx]   /∴ (x)(Dx ⊃ Rx)
       3. (Dy v Ly) ⊃ Py                         1, UI
       4. ~(Dy v Ly) v Py                        3, Impl.
       5. (~Dy·~Ly) v Py                         4, De M.
       6. Py v (~Dy · ~Ly)                       5, Com.
       7. (Py v ~Dy)·(Py v~Ly)                   6, Dist.
       8. Py v ~Dy                               7, Simp.
```

124

```
      9. ~Dy v Py                               8, Com.
     10. (~Dy v Py) v Ey                        9, Add.
     11. ~Dy v (Py v Ey)                       10, Assoc.
     12. Dy ⊃ (Py v Ey)                        11, Impl.
     13. (Py v Ey) ⊃ Ry                         2, UI
     14. Dy ⊃ Ry                               12, 13, H.S.
     15. (x)(Dx ⊃ Rx)                          14, UG
 3.  (x)[Mx ⊃ (Lx v Px)]    [Ma ⊃ (La v Pa)]
     (∃x)(Mx·~Cx)           (Ma·~Ca)
     ∴(∃x)(Lx·~Cx)          ∴(La·~Ca)
                            Ma La Pa Ca
                             t  f  t  f
 4.  1. (x)[Cx ⊃ (Sx v Ox)]
     2. (x)(Sx ⊃ ~ Wx)
     3. (∃x)(Cx·Wx)            /∴(∃x)(Cx·Ox)
     4. Ca·Wa                                   3, EI
     5. Wa·Ca                                   4, Com.
     6. Wa                                      5, Simp.
     7. Sa ⊃ ~Wa                                2, UI
     8. ~~Wa                                    6, D.N.
     9. ~Sa                                     7, 8, M.T.
    10. Ca ⊃ (Sa v Oa)                          1, UI
    11. Ca                                      4, Simp.
    12. Sa v Oa                                10, 11, M.P.
    13. Oa                                     12, 9, D.S.
    14. Ca·Oa                                  11, 13, Conj.
    15. (∃x)(Cx·Ox)                            14, EG
 6.  1. (x){[Cx·(Lx v Ox)] ⊃ ~Fx}
     2. (x)(~Fx ⊃~Ex)      /∴(x)[(Cx·Lx) ⊃ ~Ex]
     3. [Cy·(Ly v Oy)] ⊃ ~Fy                    1, UI
     4. ~Fy ⊃ ~Ey                               2, UI
     5. [Cy·(Ly v Oy)] ⊃ ~Ey                    3, 4, H.S.
     6. [(Cy·Ly) v (Cy·Oy)] ⊃ ~Ey               5, Dist.
     7. ~[(Cy·Ly) v (Cy·Oy)] v ~Ey              6, Impl.
     8. [~(Cy·Ly) · ~(Cy·Oy)] v ~Ey             7, De M.
     9. ~Ey v [~(Cy·Ly)·~(Cy·Oy)]               8, Com.
    10. [~Ey v ~(Cy·Ly)]·[~Ey v ~(Cy·Oy)]       9, Dist.
    11. ~Ey v ~(Cy·Ly)                          10, Simp.
    12. ~(Cy·Ly) v ~Ey                          11, Com.
    13. (Cy·Ly) ⊃ ~Ey                           12, Impl.
    14. (x)[(Cx·Lx) ⊃ ~Ex]                      13, UG
 7.  (x)[(Mx·Tx) ⊃ ~Fx]     [(Ma·Ta) ⊃ ~Fa]
     (x)[(Bx·Tx) ⊃ Ox]      [(Ba·Ta) ⊃ Oa]
     (∃x)[(Ax·Sx)·Bx]       [(Aa·Sa)·Ba]
     (x)(Sx ⊃ Fx)           (Sa ⊃ Fa)
     (x)(Bx ⊃ Mx)           (Ba ⊃ Ma)
     ∴(∃x)(Ax·~Ox)          ∴(Aa·~Oa)
                     Ma Ta Fa Ba Oa Aa Sa
                      t  f  t  t  t  t  t
```

125

8.   1. (x)[(Cx·Kx) ⊃ (Fx ⊃   Vx)]
      2. (x){ Cx ⊃   [Fx ≡ ~(Ix v Px)]}*
      3. (x)(Cx ⊃ Kx)
      4. (x)(Kx ⊃ ~Px)

5. (∃x)(Cx·~Vx)	/∴ (∃x)(Cx·Ix)	
6. Ca·~Va	5, EI
7. Ca ⊃ Ka	3, UI
8. Ka ⊃ ~Pa	4, UI
9. Ca	6, Simp.
10. Ka	7, 9, M.P.
11. Ca·Ka	9, 10, Conj.
12. (Ca·Ka) ⊃ (Fa ⊃ Va)	1, UI
13. Fa ⊃ Va	12, 11, M.P.
14. ~Va.Ca	6, Com.
15. ~Va	14, Simp.
16. ~Fa	13, 15, M.T.
17. Ca ⊃ [Fa ≡ ~(Ia v Pa)]	2, UI
18. Fa ≡ ~(Ia v Pa)	17, 9, M.P.
19. [Fa ⊃ ~(Ia v Pa)]·[~(Ia v Pa) ⊃ Fa]	18, Equiv.
20. [~(Ia v Pa) ⊃ Fa]·[Fa ⊃ ~(Ia v Pa)]	19, Com.
21. ~(Ia v Pa) ⊃ Fa	20, Simp.
22. ~~(Ia v Pa)	21, 16, M.T.
23. Ia v Pa	22, D.N.
24. Pa v Ia	23, Com.
25. ~Pa	8, 10, M.P.
26. Ia	24, 25, D.S.
27. Ca·Ia	9, 26, Conj.
28. (∃x)(Cx·Ix)	27, EG

9.   (x)[Bx ⊃ (Gx·Px)]
        (x){Px ⊃ [(Dx ⊃ Cx)·(Mx ⊃ Ix)]}
        (x)[(Gx·Ax) ⊃ ~Mx]
        (∃x)[Bx·(Ix·~Cx)]
        ∴(∃x)(Bx·~Ax)
        Ba ⊃ (Ga·Pa)
        Pa ⊃ [(Da ⊃ Ca)·(Ma ⊃ Ia)]
        (Ga·Aa) ⊃ ~Ma
        Ba·(Ia·~Ca)
        ∴Ba· ~Aa

Ba	Ga	Pa	Da	Ca	Ma	Ia	Aa
t	t	t	f	f	f	t	t

10. 1. (∃x)(Cx·Rx)
      2. (x)[Rx ⊃ (Sx v Bx)]
      3. (x)[Bx ⊃ (Dx v Px)]
      4. (x)(Px ⊃ Lx)
      5. (x)(Dx ⊃ Hx)

---

*   If the second premiss is interpreted differently and symbolized as (x){Cx ⊃ [~(Ix v Px) ⊃ Fx]} then the proof of validity is two steps shorter.

```
 6.  (x)(~Hx)
 7.  (x) { [(Cx·Rx)·Fx]  ⊃ Ax}
 8.  (x)(Rx  ⊃ Fx)
 9.  (x)[Cx ⊃  ~(Lx·Ax)]          /∴  (∃x)(Cx·Sx)
10.  Ca·Ra                             1, EI
11.  Ra·Ca                             10, Com.
12.  Ra                                11, Simp.
13.  Ra  ⊃ Fa                          8, UI
14.  Fa                                13, 12, M.P.
15.  (Ca·Ra)·Fa                        10, 14, Conj.
16.  [(Ca·Ra)·Fa]  ⊃ Aa                7, UI
17.  Aa                                16, 15, M.P.
18.  Ca  ⊃~(La·Aa)                     9, UI
19.  Ca                                10, Simp.
20.  ~(La·Aa)                          18, 19, M.P.
21.  ~La v ~Aa                         20, De M.
22.  ~Aa v ~La                         21, Com.
23.  Aa ⊃  ~La                         22, Impl.
24.  ~La                               23, 17, M.P.
25.  Pa ⊃ La                           4, UI
26.  ~Pa                               25, 24, M.T.
27.  Da  ⊃ Ha                          5, UI
28.  ~Ha                               6, UI
29.  ~Da                               27, 28, M.T.
30.  ~Da·~Pa                           29, 26, Conj.
31.  ~(Da v Pa)                        30, De M.
32.  Ba  ⊃ (Da v Pa)                   3, UI
33.  ~Ba                               32, 31, M.T.
34.  Ra  ⊃ (Sa v Ba)                   2, UI
35.  Sa v Ba                           34, 12, M.P.
36.  Ba v Sa                           35, Com.
37.  Sa                                36, 33, D.S.
38.  Ca·Sa                             19, 37, Conj.
39.  (∃x)(Cx·Sx)                       38, EG
11.   1.  (x)[Ex  ⊃ (Vx·Rx)]
      2.  (x)[Vx  ⊃ (Dx·Ex)]     /∴ (x)[(Vx v Ex)  ⊃ (Vx·Ex)]
      3.  Ey ⊃ (Vy·Ry)                 1, UI
      4.  ~Ey v (Vy·Ry)                3, Impl.
      5.  (~Ey v Vy)·(~Ey v Ry)        4, Dist.
      6.  ~Ey v Vy                     5, Simp.
      7.  Ey ⊃ Vy                      6, Impl.
      8.  Vy ⊃  (Dy·Ey)                2, UI
      9.  Vy ⊃  (Ey·Dy)                8, Com.
     10.  ~Vy v (Ey·Dy)                9, Impl.
     11.  (~Vy v Ey)·(~Vy v Dy)        10, Dist.
     12.  ~Vy v Ey                     11, Simp.
     13.  Vy ⊃ Ey                      12, Impl.
     14.  (Vy  ⊃ Ey)·(Ey ⊃ Vy)         13, 7, Conj.
     15.  Vy ≡ Ey                      14, Equiv.
     16.  (Vy·Ey) v (~Vy·~Ey)          15, Equiv.
     17.  (~Vy ·~Ey) v (Vy·Ey)         16, Com.
```

18. ~(Vy v Ey) v (Vy·Ey)   17, De M.
19. (Vy v Ey) ⊃ (Vy·Ey)   18, Impl.
20. (x)[(Vx v Ex) ⊃ (Vx·Ex)]   19, UG

12. 1. (x)[(Fx v Gx) ⊃ Hx]
    2. (x)[Hx ⊃ ~(Ix v Jx)]
    3. (∃x)[Gx·(Jx.Kx)]
    4. (∃x)(Fx·~Kx)   /∴ (∃x)(Fx·Ix)
    5. Ga·(Ja·Ka)
    6. Ga   3, EI
    7. Ga v Fa   5, Simp.
    8. Fa v Ga   6, Add.
    9. (Fa v Ga) ⊃ Ha   7, Com.
   10. Ha   1, UI
   11. Ha ⊃ ~(Ia v Ja)   9, 8, M.P.
   12. ~(Ia v Ja)   2, UI
   13. ~Ia·~Ja   11, 10, M.P.
   14. ~Ja·~Ia   12, De M.
   15. ~Ja   13, Com.
   16. (Ja·Ka)·Ga   14, Simp.
   17. Ja·Ka   5, Com.
   18. Ja   16, Simp.
   19. Ja v (∃x)(Fx·Ix)   17, Simp.
   20. (∃x)(Fx·Ix)   18, Add.
                           19, 15, D.S.

13. (x)[(Fx v Gx) ⊃ Hx]
   (x)[Hx ⊃ ~(Ix·Jx)]
   (∃x)[Gx· (Jx·Kx)]
   (∃x)(Fx ·~Kx)
   ∴(∃x)(Fx ·~Ix)
   [(Fa v Ga) ⊃ Ha]·[(Fb v Gb) ⊃ Hb]
   [Ha ⊃ ~(Ia·Ja)]·[Hb ⊃ ~(Ib·Jb)]
   [Ga·(Ja·Ka)] v [Gb·(Jb·Kb)]
   (Fa·~Ka) v (Fb·~Kb)
   ∴(Fa·~Ia) v (Fb·~Ib)

Fa	Fb	Ga	Gb	Ha	Hb	Ia	Ib	Ja	Jb	Ka	Kb
t	f	t	t	t	t	t	f	f	t	f	t

or numerous other truth value assignments.

14. 1. (x)(Gx ⊃ Vx)
    2. (x)(Rx ⊃ Ox)   /∴ (x)[(Gx·Rx) ⊃ (Vx·Ox)]
    3. Gy ⊃ Vy   1, UI
    4. Ry ⊃ Oy   2, UI
    5. ~Gy v Vy   3, Impl.
    6. (~Gy v Vy) v ~Ry   5, Add.
    7. ~Gy v (Vy v ~Ry)   6, Assoc.
    8. ~Gy v (~Ry v Vy)   7, Com.
    9. (~Gy v ~Ry) v Vy   8, Assoc.
   10. ~Ry v Oy   4, Impl.
   11. (~Ry v Oy) v ~Gy   10, Add.
   12. ~Gy v (~Ry v Oy)   11, Com.
   13. (~Gy v ~Ry) v Oy   12, Assoc.
   14. [(~Gy v ~Ry) v Vy]·[(~Gy v ~Ry) v Oy]   9, 13, Conj.
   15. (~Gy v ~Ry) v (Vy·Oy)   14, Dist.

16. ~(Gy·Ry) v (Vy·Oy)   15, De M.
17. (Gy·Ry) ⊃ (Vy·Oy)   16, Impl.
18. (x)[(Gx·Rx) ⊃ (Vx·Ox)]   17, UG

15.
1. (x)(Ox ⊃ Sx)
2. (x)(Lx ⊃ Tx)   /∴ (x)[(Ox v Lx) ⊃ (Sx v Tx)]
3. Oy ⊃ Sy   1, UI
4. Ly ⊃ Ty   2, UI
5. ~Oy v Sy   3, Impl.
6. (~Oy v Sy) v Ty   5, Add.
7. ~Oy v (Sy v Ty)   6, Assoc.
8. (Sy v Ty) v ~Oy   7, Com.
9. ~Ly v Ty   4, Impl.
10. (~Ly v Ty) v Sy   9, Add.
11. ~Ly v (Ty v Sy)   10, Assoc.
12. ~Ly v (Sy v .Ty)   11, Com.
13. (Sy v Ty) v ~Ly   12, Com.
14. [(Sy v Ty) v ~Oy].[(Sy v Ty) v ~Ly]   8, 13, Conj.
15. (Sy v Ty) v (~Oy·~Ly)   14, Dist.
16. (~Oy· ~Ly) v (Sy v Ty)   15, Com.
17. ~(Oy v Ly) v (Sy v Ty)   16, De M.
18. (Oy v Ly) ⊃ (Sy v Ty)   17, Impl.
19. (x)[(Ox v Lx) ⊃ (Sx v Tx)]   18, UG

Exercises on pages 380-385

2. Nonargumentative use of analogy. 3. Analogical argument. 4. Nonargumentative use of analogy. 6. Analogical argument. 7. Nonargumentative use of analogy. 8. Analogical argument. 9. Nonargumentative use of analogy. 11. Nonargumentative use of analogy. 12. Analogical argument. 13. Can be regarded either as an analogical argument or as a refutation by logical analogy of the sort discussed in Sections 6.2, 8.4, and 10.5. 14. Nonargumentative use of analogy. 16. Nonargumentative use of analogy. 17. Analogical argument. 18. Nonargumentative use of analogy. 19. Analogical argument. 21. Analogical argument. 22. Analogical argument. (In its context it is a refutation by logical analogy.) 23. Nonargumentative use of analogy. 24. Analogical argument.

Exercises on pages 390-392

I. 2. a - less, b - more, c - neither, d - more, e - more, f - more.
3. a - more, b - neither, c - more, d - more, e - more, f - less.
4. a - more, b - more, c - less, d - more, e - neither (or possibly more if Bill knows that he is more alert and/or appreciative early in the morning than at other times of the day), f - more (because they are all social sciences).
5. a - more, b - less, c - more, d - neither, e - more, f - more.

Exercises on pages 518-519

2(a). 1/2,197   2(b). 1/5,525   3(a). 2,560,000/20,151,121

3(b). 703/5,896   4. 1/10,077,696   6. 1/25
7. .536096484   8. 1/358,800   9. flush (probability
9/47 vs. 8/47 for straight)   10. Put 50 black balls and
49 white balls in one urn, 1 white ball in the other urn
to make probability of 2 white balls 49/99.

Exercises on pages 523-524
2(a). 1 - 27/64 = 37/64   2(b). 1 - 703/1700 = 997/1700
3. 1 - 1/8 = 7/8   4(a). 1/6   4(b). 117/812   6(a). 1/70
6(b). 1/35   6(c). 1/14   6(d). 11/70   6(e). 1/210
6(f). 1/21   6(g). 11/105   6(h). 1/21   6(i). 11/42
6(j). 11/42   7(a). .948658   7(b). .354316   8. 43/60;
if in one case then 8/11   9. 2/47 + 60/1,081 + 6/1,081 =
112/1,081   10. 3/11; if ace of spades is announced then
3/7

Exercises on pages 529-530
2. $5.52   3. $7/9 (78¢)   4. $9/11 (82¢)   6. The
favorite: $1 bet on him purchases an expectation of 92¢
($1 bet on the dark horse purchases an expectation of only
90¢).   7. the common stock: $100 spent on common pur-
chases an expectation of $93.80, whereas $100 spent on the
preferred purchases an expectation of only $93.50.
8. 2 1/2¢   9. $499   10. $7   11. 1/6

L

ISBN 0-02-324890-4